BEYOND APPLAUSE

Make a
MEANINGFUL DIFFERENCE
through
TRANSFORMATIONAL
SPEAKING

MICHELLE BARRY FRANCO

Brilliance at Work
Forest Knolls, CA 94933

Published 2018
ISBN-13: 978-0-9996702-2-4

Cover Design: David Provolo
Editor: Kelly Lydick
Author's photo courtesy of Sophia Mavrides
Interior Design: Adina Cucicov

Dedication

This book is dedicated to my beautiful, heart-driven clients who have taught me what it means to throw fear and uncertainty to the wind, and step into the bright light of service through sharing their powerful stories, life lessons, and expertise.

TABLE OF CONTENTS

INTRODUCTION

*W*e were standing outside of Grace's gorgeously designed office after a talk I delivered for her organization. As our conversation started to wrap up, she leaned in and whispered to me. "You know, I'd really love to do more speaking. I've always imagined myself on a big stage inspiring hundreds of women, kind of like a female version of Tony Robbins."

Delighted to be in on the secret, I asked, "What's stopping you?"

"I don't know how to get on those bigger stages. I even know people who are part of these big events, and I've gotten warm introductions to meeting organizers, but that doesn't seem to be enough. How does a person get on those kinds of stages?"

I realized as she was talking that this is one of the most frequent questions I'm asked as a speaking coach: "How do I get the kind of speaking opportunities that help me make the biggest difference with my message?"

I'm asked this question even more than: "How do I craft and deliver a great speech?"

This particular conversation with Grace was an epiphany for me. For the past two decades, my primary focus has been helping my clients and students craft and deliver compelling and captivating talks and presentations. Makes sense, right? That's what speaking coaches and teachers do.

But in this moment, I realized that I had been focusing on only half of the process.

Grace's whispered secret that day outside her office—and the pointed follow-up question—expressed the deepest desire of my very best clients. They are already very good speakers. They care deeply about making an impact, so they invest in a speaking coach to become an even better speaker. But what they really want is to contribute in a meaningful way to the larger conversation in their topic area. They want to have influence and create positive change for as many people as possible. They want to be a part of the highest-level conversation in their industry. They know that many of those conversations happen at the most respected gatherings in their industries—conferences, summits, symposiums—and they want to be on those stages with other influencers.

They don't want to just be great speakers—they want to be "go-to" thought leaders in their industry so they can make the biggest difference with their message.

It's not just about being a great speaker—it's about being a "go-to" thought leader in your industry to make the biggest difference with your message.

As recognized thought leaders, their stories and cutting-edge ideas will be at the forefront of their industry, allowing them to bring real change to the lives of many people who are seeking solutions.

Their desire to be on bigger stages is driven not by the desire to be "famous" or a love of the spotlight (though some are very happy on stage), the desire is driven by a passion for making a difference in the lives of others. They have learned powerful lessons and they know that their stories will inspire and change lives. They are on a mission to share those stories and life lessons and to make the impact they know they are meant to make for others.

This realization sent me down an enlightening path of research and insight. I went back to my office and made a list of all my clients and most active speaking students. I reviewed notes about our sessions together, their struggles and learning, and what they were doing with their message now, often many years after I began working with them. I took inventory of where they were speaking, how often, and any other ways they were contributing to the public conversation in their topic area.

I also began studying some of my favorite speakers who were speaking on the most influential stages, and asked: "How did they get on those stages? How is their approach different than others who aren't offered these kinds of opportunities?"

What I found in these inquiries immediately changed the focus of my work and is the basis of this book. When I thought about all of my beautiful clients and their deep desire to serve as a speaker, like Grace, I felt my own "fire-in-the-belly" rise. They must be out in our world, serving far and wide with their message. *You* must be out in our world, serving with *your* message.

WHY IT'S WORTH IT TO BECOME A GO-TO SPEAKER IN YOUR INDUSTRY

Some of us are called to share our stories and expertise as a speaker. It's a gut level feeling, a visceral drive to serve in this specific way. After more than thirty years in the speaking world, I know this as an absolute truth.

What I also know from this many years in the speaking world is that this pull to speak—this fire-in-the-belly drive—is persistent. It doesn't go away, even when you try to ignore it. There is very real pain, and significant personal price, when we ignore this call to serve. You will read my own story about this in the pages ahead.

However, when you do decide to answer this call to share your story and message, and commit to serving fully in this way, the payoff can be incredible. The feeling of satisfaction and purpose is magnificent. Suddenly, that internal drive that often felt edgy and scary becomes a feeling of deep alignment with your life's purpose. I believe this alignment with your purpose is the most valuable reason to become a go-to speaker in your industry. The difference you want to make through sharing your message is at the heart of your desire to speak, and therefore the fact that real lives will be changed through your thought leadership speaking is immensely valuable and gratifying.

In fact, there is no more powerful way to serve a lot of people all at once than through high-impact speaking. When you craft and deliver a talk that captivates and motivates your audience to positive action, you change lives. Your stories give people hope and inspiration. Your lessons learned help them make different choices—or know what to do if things go awry on their own path. One of the greatest gifts that one human can give to another is the feeling of not being alone—and your courageous sharing will give them that experience.

Speaking on bigger stages allows you to have an impact on the lives in the room, yes, but the ripple effect is also strong and meaningful. The people in your audience, they go home, and if your talks are inspiring enough, and there's enough sharable content, they share that with their families and their friends. Those family and friends may even share those stories further. Your impact often reaches much further than you can see.

It's possible the greatest impact of this kind of speaking is on ourselves. I remember leaping from my seat in the audience and racing to the green room area after Gail finished her TEDx talk. Seeing the giddy delight dancing across her face was magical. In fact, she was actually dancing around the room she was so excited. When you push yourself to the edges of your own brilliance, you meet a part of yourself that you are often seeking, but rarely get to engage. In this moment, I was seeing this truth in action on Gail's face.

When you push yourself to the edges of your own brilliance, you meet a part of yourself that you are often seeking, but rarely get to engage.

An avid skydiver in years past, just as she was about to go on stage, Gail said: "This feels exactly like I'm about to skydive!" I love this analogy because that mix of exhilaration and fear is characteristic of the moments before a high-stakes talk. It also makes a perfect connection between the very real fear that can come with sharing our stories and lessons learned on a stage, and the *actual* risk of dying that comes with skydiving. As far as I know, no one has ever died as a direct result of public speaking. Sadly, we can't say that about skydiving. Yet, the feelings in our bodies as we anticipate both are so similar. It's a fascinating truth, which we explore more deeply in Chapter 15 on Releasing Fear.

The other amazing thing that happened with Gail as a result of stepping into thought leadership speaking is that the very next weekend she finally launched an official speaking website so that she could do a whole lot more speaking—something she had been dreaming about for years. When you meet yourself at the edge of what you're capable of, as Gail did that day on the TEDx stage, you become a new and better version of yourself. That's a pretty awesome reason to get on those bigger stages.

If you have financial reasons as part of your speaking goals, then high-impact speaking is also an excellent business growth strategy. I'll never forget my first speaking gig on behalf of my business. It seems so naive now, but when I stood up in front of that room full of people, I wasn't focused on attracting a lot of clients through my talk. I wanted to share information about my new business and test out my ideas. When one of the most influential women in the room handed me her business card and said, "Call me," as I was walking back to my seat, I realized how effective speaking was as a natural client attraction strategy. The fact is, most of my best clients come as a result of my own thought leadership speaking.

Of course, you can also get paid nicely to speak. For one of my earlier books, I interviewed Chris Brogan, who is a popular business speaker and online business mentor. He told me a story about how he was charging $2,800 for a keynote speech in his early speaking days. One night after he delivered a talk at an industry event, he passed Guy Kawasaki, another well-respected business speaker and mentor, in the backstage area. As they passed one another, Guy said, "Hey, I just gave your name to a company that was looking for a speaker. Charge them a lot of money!" Chris turned around and said, "What do you mean by a lot of money?" Guy said, "Charge them $25,000." Chris was stunned at this idea, but when he got on the call and they asked what his rate was, he said, "$22,000." Chris went from $2,800 per speech to $22,000 per speech in just one phone call.

Whether you are looking for paid speaking opportunities or not, thoughtfully planned speaking to the right audiences (which we cover in this book) is an excellent business or mission-growing strategy.

THE SHADOW SIDE OF THE CALL TO SERVE WITH YOUR MESSAGE

We are each made for contribution. We, human beings, are meaning-making machines. When you are called to contribute through sharing your voice, the fulfillment of that calling is not only meaningful for your life purpose, but it also supports your own well-being. Authentic, powerful self-expression is an essential part of living a whole-hearted life.

> Authentic, powerful self-expression is an essential part of living a whole-hearted life.

There is a shadow side to this truth. As Brené Brown famously says, "Unused creativity is not benign. It metastasizes. It turns into grief, rage, judgment, sorrow, shame." The pull in our hearts to share our stories and lessons learned is an expression of that creativity within us. Not every person feels this tug—creativity lives in each of us in unique ways—but for those of us who are called to speak, the pull is undeniable.

This visceral call to serve can also have a high price if it's ignored. Brené Brown's quote speaks to this truth. I've seen it over and over again with clients who have tried to turn away from their calling. In fact, I experienced it in my own life profoundly.

I've been called to serve through my stories and expertise for as long as I can remember but I didn't answer that call fully for many years. Instead, I did this dance of "shiny sharing" where I'd share just enough to create connection but not so much as to make me feel vulnerable. Being vulnerable is scary, after all. I knew I was living and working in a protected way. It was impossible to be in full denial of my own lack of authenticity when my job is guiding others into their full expression. I just didn't know how to move through the fear. In fact, I wasn't even fully aware of the degree to which fear was blocking my own full expression. In so many ways I was just like my clients, only I couldn't figure out how to coach myself through this giant brick wall in my own expression. So, I kept ignoring it— telling myself that my focus was supposed to be on my clients' full expression, not necessarily my own.

Read that quote from Brené Brown one more time and you'll see exactly why this didn't work for me. It doesn't work for anyone, and I'm certainly no exception. As a result of ignoring my own internal call to share my message and stories, I was feeling and living out all of those emotions that Brené Brown describes: grief, rage, judgment, sorrow, shame. That's a whole lot of pain to hold in one sensitive heart, mind and body and it was definitely more than I knew how to handle. I did what many of us do when we don't have healthy ways of dealing with intense emotions. I drank too much, ate too much and blamed others for my misery. These coping mechanisms weren't only detrimental to my health, they also threatened my marriage, my friendships, my relationship with my daughters and my work. This is embarrassing to share, but also an important part of my message now. I had to go through a deep reckoning with my own authentic expression to make the impact I have felt called to make my whole life. It was the most important thing I've ever done in service of my life calling— and for my marriage and family.

Your story doesn't have to be as deep and dark as mine in order to recognize ways in which a lack of full expression may be blocking your greatest life. In fact, the simple truth that in spite of your deep desire to serve, you might never know what you are capable of as a speaker and leader is fully reason enough to make this commitment to serve with your message.

Becoming a recognized leader and speaker in your industry and sharing your voice with more people allows you to create at the edges of your own self-expression. It teaches you what you're made of when the stakes are high, when fear is threatening to shut you down. You learn that you can do hard things—things that scare you—in service of making a difference.

WHAT GETS IN THE WAY OF BECOMING THE SPEAKER YOU KNOW YOU'RE MEANT TO BE

At this point, hopefully you're thinking, "Okay—I'm convinced! It's time for me to finally do what it takes to share my message and my stories in a bigger way."

You might also be thinking—"Actually, I've been trying to do this already—for a long time. I need to know *how* to do this if I'm ever going to make the difference I'm supposed to make."

This is the crux of the problem, isn't it? Desire to get on these awesome stages isn't enough. It gets you on the path but it doesn't keep you there. What keeps you on the path is commitment to the long game, and willingness to do what it takes to establish leadership as a speaker. It also takes knowing exactly what steps to take on that path.

The fact is, getting the kind of speaking opportunities that allow you to make a broad-reaching impact is difficult. A small percentage of people in any industry are invited to be a part of those highest-level conversations from the stage, which means the path to getting there is competitive. Event and conference organizers need to bring to their stages people who they know their audiences will love—the best in their industry. That way, the audience returns again next time with all of their friends. There are essentially three ways to get on these bigger stages.

1. Already be famous. Like, Tony Robbins, Brené Brown, or Sheryl Sandberg (all who had smaller stages first, by the way).
2. Do something so remarkable that audiences will be lining up out the door to come hear your story. Emergency landing an airplane full of people on a small body of water and saving hundreds of lives, or being the first to bake chocolate chip cookies from your space ship on the moon (which essentially bumps you into number one above) are some examples.
3. Consistently and powerfully serve your audience (of whatever size) with your life-changing message. If you do this, over time you will create the opportunity to move up to those bigger stages.

If you read this over closely, you see that one and three are essentially the same, just at different stages of career progression. In almost all cases, number two also takes many years of systematic learning and commitment.

You must become known for a message that matters and consistently take a stand for that message in your speaking.

So, as unsexy as it is, the way to get on those bigger stages is to decide now that you are going to be the most compelling, engaging speaker and thought leader possible. The difference you make for the people in your audience and the clarity, conviction and impact of your message are what make you the kind of speaker that event organizers seek. You must become known for a message that matters and consistently take a stand for that message in your speaking.

In fact, this is the beginning of the path to getting on the best stages in your industry so you can make the biggest difference possible.

TRANSFORMATIONAL THOUGHT LEADERSHIP

The exciting news is, there does seem to be a "path" to becoming a "go-to" speaker in your industry and getting on more influential stages. That path is paved through a commitment to *serving* others. This commitment is about more than just being a captivating and inspiring speaker. It's about serving the audience in the speaking room and beyond—inspiring them to change their lives in meaningful ways. It's about a full-hearted commitment to making a powerful difference in other people's lives and in our world.

This kind of speaking is a leadership move. It's a decision to step into the spotlight, over and over again, even when it's scary and hard, with the sole purpose of impact. I have come to call this kind of leadership *Transformational Thought Leadership* and it includes your thought leadership speaking as well as other forms of sharing your expertise and lessons learned, such as published books and articles and expert interviews. You will see this term used with some variations in the public discourse as it is rising in popularity. For our purposes, this is our definition.

> This kind of speaking is a leadership move. It's a decision to step into the spotlight, over and over again, even when it's scary and hard, with the sole purpose of impact.

This fancy set of words feels a bit intellectual for such a heart-driven mission as changing lives. And yet, each word is perfectly accurate for this mission you are on. You are committed to changing lives, transforming them into something better in ways the audience desires (transformational). To make this difference, you are sharing your very best ideas (thought). You are courageously standing in front of rooms full of people, offering to show them the way to making their life better (leadership). See what I mean? Transformational Thought Leadership.

Okay, so the case is made for Transformational Thought Leadership and its power to set you up as a go-to speaker in your industry so that you can make the difference you are called to make. The next logical and pressing question is:

How do you step into Transformational Thought Leadership?

This is where I get to lay out for you the simple, yet oh-so-powerful Path to Thought Leadership, which is also the framework for this book.

THE PATH TO THOUGHT LEADERSHIP

1. Take a stand for something that matters.
2. Commit to serve through that stand.
3. Go where they gather and serve.

I will walk you through every step of this model, including action steps in every section, throughout this book. To give you a sense of where we are going, here's a summary of each of these steps.

Take a Stand for a Message that Matters

At the heart of your greatest impact is a clear and powerful message that matters in the lives of others. It's the stand you take, based on your expertise and experience. This experience is often quite personal, and is at the heart of your Story of Transformation. The process of clarifying this stand includes understanding who you are meant to serve with this message. This essential element of Transformational Thought Leadership can be the hardest part and takes the deepest work. Once you have this clarified, however, you can be unstoppable in your impact in our world.

Commit to Serve Through That Stand

Once you have your message and ideal audience clarified, it's time to turn that message into ways that you make a meaningful difference for those you are meant to serve. For our purposes, the focus is on captivating, inspiring speaking. Serving at the highest level as a thought leader, however, includes all of the ways that you can reach out to and serve your audience. This includes publishing articles and books, providing interviews and many other forms of making a difference. The most important element in this phase of The Path to Leadership is your commitment to doing the work to serve your ideal audience members consistently and for the long haul.

Go Where They Gather and Serve

The people you are meant to serve with your message are already gathering in person and online to try to solve the problems that they uniquely share. As a speaker, speaking at these events is the most powerful and gratifying way to serve with your message. However, there are many ways to serve your audience beyond speaking. In fact, committing to serve even when you are not a speaker at an event can be an excellent strategy for eventually being invited to speak on the most exciting stages. The focus in this phase of The Path to Thought Leadership is service. Service means making a difference while you are speaking in the room—or virtual space—and afterward as well, including gracefully and naturally attracting potential new clients.

The Path to Thought Leadership model is so simple, it could be easy to dismiss. Don't let it fool you, though. This simple path is the action plan for answering that call you feel to make the difference you are devoted to making with your message.

There are real people out there who are feeling afraid and alone. Their struggles are blocking their ability to live the lives they dream of living. Your story—and the lessons you've learned—could be exactly what they need to know that they are not alone, and that there is hope for a way to get to the other side of their struggle.

You know this—and now you have the plan to serve them in the most powerful way through speaking. Hooray!

But wait—let's take one more moment to check in here. Sometimes at this point in the process with clients, when they get a clear overall picture of their potential role as a leader in their industry, they begin to question their readiness. Some of this is very natural fear (see more on how to deal with this part in the next section) and the other part of this questioning is an appropriate assessment process. They wonder if they have enough experience or training, or if their stories are dramatic enough. In case this is happening for you, know this: that call you feel within you is your sign that you are meant to step into leadership. The additional good news is, this book will guide you to step into that role for the *right people* with the *right message* with full heart and soul.

Your story doesn't have to be dramatic, it just needs to be honest and crafted in a way that serves the right people who need to hear it. Your level of experience and training and expertise is perfectly aligned with a particular audience. This book will guide you in choosing the right audience and sharing your expertise and story in the most useful way for that audience.

> Your story doesn't have to be dramatic, it just needs to be honest and crafted in a way that serves the right people who need to hear it.

You're here because you are ready to serve in a big and meaningful way through your speaking. You know that you are meant to be a beacon of light for others who are looking for a way to get to the other side of that struggle. I know you are meant to be a beacon of light, too. I'm honored and thrilled that I get to show you a path to making the difference you feel called to make with your message by stepping into Transformational Thought Leadership.

Up until now, there's been no guide for how to step into transformational thought leadership, move onto the most influential stages and make the biggest difference with your message. But that's changed because here we are: you, me, this book, and the message you have that's ready to change lives.

Let's do this!

Oh, wait... one more (pretty important) thing...

A NOTE ABOUT FEAR

Before we go any further, we've got to address the number one obstacle to big, influential, highly-visible work: Fear.

It may surprise you to know that some of the most anxious public speaking clients I've had are high-level leaders of companies. They are confident, powerful, smart, driven people who are used to being successful. Yet when it comes to speaking—especially speaking that includes personal stories and lessons learned—they feel very anxious. When you think about it, this makes sense. They are used to a shiny exterior; to being respected for their success and ideas. This is what was going on for me in the story I shared earlier about my own blocked expression. Great speaking that moves people almost always includes vulnerability, sharing stories of falling down and figuring out how to get back up. These leaders are unaccustomed to sharing these kinds of stories. They are nervous because they care—yes, about their reputation, but in my experience—even more about making an impact and influencing their audiences positively.

As you know, every successful person's journey holds many moments of risk, uncertainty, and failure. When you have built success in your life, one of the tricky things about fear is that you become accustomed to turning away from it—often simply ignoring it—and therefore may not realize that it lingers in the background affecting your behavior.

Fear is stealthy. It doesn't always present itself in obvious ways: racing heart, sweaty palms, spinning thoughts. Sometimes it appears as "Ah, this is no big deal" and "I've got this, I don't need to prepare." As a confident leader already, you're used to performing under pressure and often in stressful circumstances. You likely have some excellent, almost automatic strategies for ignoring fear. This is valuable to note as we venture into this work together. You may need to dig a little deeper when resistance shows up in order to release fear that might be driving that resistance. (I devote a whole chapter toward the end of this book to releasing fear, which includes some of my best anxiety-releasing strategies.)

For now, let's just take note that fear is likely to be a natural part of your commitment to serving at this level, with this kind of visibility. And let's not let it get in the way of working through the proven process laid out ahead.

Because it's time to step in, my friend! Let's do this! (For real this time.)

MAKE THE MOST OF THIS BOOK

Be sure to take full advantage of the many additional resources on the book resources page located at **beyondapplausebook. com/resources**. In that area, you'll find templates, guides, checklists—so many resources that will help you take committed action on what you create through the contents of this book. The resources on that page are at no cost to you. When you register to access that page, you will also automatically receive updates on book content and my almost-weekly newsletter through which I share my best ideas for serving our world as a transformational thought leader.

Get yourself a journal you love to use with this book. There are many exercises that will lead to notes and outcomes you will want to reference. Keep that journal and a favorite pen handy whenever you are reading this book.

TAKE A STAND

for

SOMETHING
THAT MATTERS

Chapter One

THE STAND AT THE CENTER OF YOUR WORK

*I*n Liz Gilbert's "Magic Lessons with Elizabeth Gilbert" podcast, she interviewed Glennon Doyle Melton. Glennon shares a story of how she promised herself after she got sober that she'd tell the whole truth out loud in her life. No more hiding. This was the complete opposite of how she was living before, and it was the only way she could think of to help stay on track with sobriety. To honor this commitment, every day she wrote about her life as a wife and mother and how we can do hard things and published those posts on her blog. That blog of a few readers turned into hundreds, and then thousands. Today, Glennon speaks regularly on stages, podcasts and interviews in many of the high-level venues where women gather to support each other in feeling good inside their lives.

Glennon is now a "go-to" thought leader committed to helping women live lives of wholeness. She takes a stand for women, their voices and their contributions in our world—even when life gets hard and doesn't go the way we imagined. Two of her key mantras are, "We can do hard things" and "Love wins."

An example of a "stand that matters" in the education and business realm is Sir Ken Robinson. An academic for a long time with an early career as a university professor, he describes a warm and respectful relationship with academia overall. And yet, his 2006 TED Talk—one of the most-watched TED talks of all time as of this writing—is titled "Do Schools Kill Creativity?" This is an especially intriguing question, given his connection with academia.

Sir Ken Robinson did not start out as a renowned thought leader, speaking on the coveted TED stage about creativity in education and business. He started with smaller projects, closer to home. He made an impact on smaller stages, tested his ideas, explored new questions, and learned. Over time, he began to take a stand for his ideas about the need for more creative expression for our children in public schools. Eventually, his innovative ideas caught the attention of TED organizers because he was sharing them with conviction and competence, in a captivating way.

When a business or high-level conference is looking for a speaker on the topic of creativity and its value and impact on success—in school or work—there's a good chance Sir Ken Robinson is on the very short list of desired keynote speakers.

In these examples you can see the clear stand these thought leaders take, as well as the evolution of their path to being a recognized thought leader. Very rarely does a person come out the gate being invited on popular podcasts like "Magic Lessons with Elizabeth Gilbert" or, even more coveted, as a TED main-stage speaker.

You'll notice that this first step of The Path to Thought Leadership includes two parts:

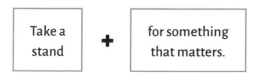

Each of these parts is essential to your success in taking your stand.

TAKING A STAND...

The very core of your contribution as a thought leader and speaker is the stand you take through your speaking. This stand is the thing you feel most compelled to say, what I call your Rooftop Message. We are going to dive into how to reveal the stand you take in the next chapter. For now, the important thing to know is that the clarity and conviction of your stand is at the heart of your ability to serve as a thought leader.

> The clarity and conviction of your stand is at the heart of your ability to serve as a thought leader.

This may seem straight forward, but it is the most common mistake that I see aspiring speakers make. Instead of proactively claiming the one thing for which they are known, they offer a variety of topics upon which they can speak. Or worse, speakers ask meeting organizers to give them a topic about which the organizer would like them to speak.

This lack of a clear stand causes a number of problems for speakers:

1. The speaker is often asked to speak on a topic that doesn't light them up, resulting in a less than excellent content and delivery experience.
2. Potential future speaking opportunities that could arise from this speaking event are less likely to transpire because the speaker isn't working in their most exciting and passionate topic area.
3. Potential clients and event planners for future speaking opportunities are confused about their stand and expertise.
4. Many possible client relationships that may have grown from this speaking opportunity are lost because the audience doesn't feel that intuitive resonance with the message, and the stories don't indicate

to them that this speaker is a meaningful solution to their current struggle.

The solution to all of this lost opportunity is to get crystal clear on the stand you take as a transformational thought leader and then offer talks *only* in that topic area.

A word of caution here: as you become known and enjoyed as a speaker, colleagues and friends will ask you to speak on topics that stray from the stand you take. This happens to my clients all the time. Unless you love to speak on a separate topic for purely cause-related reasons (and even then, be sure you know your story about why you speak on this topic and share it often), I strongly advise you not to agree to these speaking opportunities. Instead, if you feel compelled to speak for this audience, offer an alternate talk that will meet the needs of the audience and is also aligned with the stand you take.

Recently one of my clients who is the founder of a fast-growing company was invited to speak at a conference on a topic outside of her stand. She simply responded with enthusiasm to serve the audience and offered the topics she speaks on at conferences that this particular audience would most enjoy. It turns out the meeting organizer wasn't attached to the particular topic she proposed so much as she was trying to make it an easy "yes" for my client about the speaking opportunity. Within a few email exchanges, they had agreed on a talk that was aligned with my client's stand and would delight and serve the audience gathering at this conference.

Becoming known as a thought leader in your topic area requires you to stay true and consistent with your message via the crystal clear stand you take. In the next chapter, you will clarify your stand so you are ready for any opportunities coming your way.

...FOR SOMETHING THAT MATTERS

This is where things get even more exciting. You can take a stand all day long but if no one cares about that stand, you'll be standing there talking to the fire hydrants (don't worry, we won't let this happen to you).

While I focus a great deal in this book on what your Ideal Audience Members need and want, the truth is the focus on their desires must be second to what you are *called to say*. So, the first place that your stand must matter is with *you*. (We will cover this in more detail in the next chapter.)

The place your stand will make the biggest difference, of course, is out in the world serving audiences. This is where you must be exceedingly clear about who you are meant to serve with this stand, and why it matters to them.

It is the combination of the stand you take and the deep understanding of how your stand will change lives that makes your thought leadership so transformational.

Here are examples of Stands That Matter:

- Children should not sit all day long at school. They need to move their bodies to learn and be well.
- A man should not have to miss his kids' childhoods while he grows his career.
- Self-portraiture is a fast path to personal insight and growth. Take selfies!
- Families should sit down to dinner together as often as possible—it makes kids and adults resilient and strong.
- Teenagers become compassionate and loving people when they get to explore the world. Take them on trips as much as possible!

The options for stands one could take are endless. It also becomes quite obvious how the "that matters" part depends largely on the audience and what they need and want. As you can see in these examples, each of these stands is designed to serve a particular audience. One audience is parents of teens being encouraged to take their kids traveling (this could be adapted for educators as well). The stand that men should not have to miss their kids' childhoods is ideal for a men's conference, and possibly even a business conference or a special-focus conference on balance inside of a large corporation.

People often express concern about taking a stand and then changing their mind as their life experience shifts and new ideas come to life. Of course your stand will evolve and shift over time. The key is to get crystal clear on one stand you are passionate about for this next phase of time, and become known as a thought leader on behalf of that stand. Treat it like a mission in the world. It becomes so natural for you to be the one invited to speak on stages that serve the audiences that need your message. If and when you feel yourself losing passion for that stand, or another important stand rises up, spend time going through this book with that new stand in mind. You will know when it is right for you to shift.

Chapter Two

YOUR ROOFTOP MESSAGE

*I*magine that you are in a quaint little town and the streets are full of people. These people are struggling with something you know how to help them solve. They're all talking with each other about the struggle, and trying to figure out what to do. There's a heaviness and a chattering chaos. You think: "Oh my gosh, I can help these people. How can I tell them?" Then, you see a building, and leaning up against this building is a ladder that leads up to a reasonably flat roof. You walk over to this ladder and climb the steps onto the rooftop. Standing on the rooftop, you lean toward the crowd, hands cupped around your mouth, and shout: "Listen to me beautiful people! I can help you. Here is what you need to know..."

What would you say to them next to help make their lives better?

This is your "Rooftop Message."

Your Rooftop Message is the thing that you want to shout from the rooftops because you see people struggling with it everywhere. You know how hard that struggle is—often because you've been there yourself—and you've helped so many other people move through that struggle. Your heart calls out to them and you want to say, "Let me help you. You don't have to struggle like this."

This Rooftop Message is at the center of the stand you take in your thought leadership.

Let me share some examples of Rooftop Messages for some of the popular personal development and business thought leaders today. I think you'll be able to see how easy it is to know what they take a stand for just by listening to their public discussions, talks, books, interviews, and talk shows.

Oprah Winfrey: *You are meant to live your best life.*

Brendon Burchard: *High performance is a habit we can create for ourselves*

Tara Mohr: *Women, use your voices. Play bigger in the ways your heart calls to you to do so, because we need your contributions in our world!*

Donald Miller: *If you confuse, you lose—your message clarity is critical to business success.*

Brené Brown: *Take the risk, be vulnerable, because that's where we experience our greatest life. And be very selective about whose opinions you take to heart.*

As you can see in these examples, I simply extracted the core message from their talks and their other contributions as thought leaders. Each of these is an example of a clear stand for an idea through their thought leadership. That's what you want: this kind of clarity and recognition for the stand that you take with your thought leadership. Your Rooftop Message will be the center, the core of that stand.

Here are some examples from some of my clients' Rooftop Messages.

Monique, a functional nutritionist in the Philippines who works with expats would say: "Care for your gut, and you'll feel so much better. You are miserable because your gut health is off-balance. You can fix this. Let me help you."

Anna, a life and career transitions coach, would shout: "You do not have to be miserable at work. I promise you there are things you can do in your current job that will radically change your daily experience."

Jane, a filmmaker and director, wants her fellow creatives to know: "You can call in the muse any time with some simple actions. This is going to make your creative life so much less stressful and a lot more fun. It did mine."

Your Rooftop Message doesn't have to be fancy, or buttoned up, or perfect in any way. After all, you just climbed up that ladder because you saw a problem that you can solve and you were moved to solve it fast.

Here's the other thing that will help you do this exercise with more ease: your Rooftop Message will change. You're not tethered to this message. In fact, it is appropriate that your Rooftop Message changes as you learn through serving audiences and clients with your message. So go ahead and get started. Take a stand for the things you'd want to get up on that rooftop and shout. Then let's start getting you out there serving audiences with this stand and learning how you can say it even better to make an even bigger impact over time.

Now it's your turn. Let's articulate Your Rooftop Message. Let me ask you the question again, anew:

You are standing in a town full of people. The streets are overflowing with chaos and uncertainty. Everyone is talking at once, struggling to solve the very problem that you know how to solve—the one that's at the heart of your own message, the stand you want to take in the world.

You look around for a way to get their attention, but there's too much going on. You can't reach them all.

Then you see that ladder against a building—with a rooftop safe enough for you to stand on. You walk over to and climb up that ladder. You lean over the edge of the rooftop and shout: "Listen to me beautiful people! Here's what you need to know to solve the problem you are struggling with right now..."

What would you say from that rooftop? Write that in your journal and dog-ear or bookmark that page. You'll be referencing it often.

Congratulations! You've got your own Rooftop Message!

Chapter Three

YOUR IDEAL AUDIENCE MEMBER

*W*e had been on the phone for about 15 minutes exploring her Rooftop Message when I asked my client the next most important question to get clear on her thought leadership stand.

"Okay, who is on the streets of your town? Who do you want to serve with this awesome message of yours?"

"Well, everyone needs to know this!" she said.

I suspected this was coming. Mostly because she was right—everyone does need to understand that what we eat dramatically impacts the way we feel every single day. I had zero argument with that. I've had the gift of working with enough nutritionists and holistic health professionals to be completely convinced of this truth.

And yet, I persisted because I know that "everyone" won't listen at once.

"I know that everyone needs to hear this, but you can't speak to everyone in a compelling way at once, so you have to choose one Ideal Audience Member whom you can most impact, the one Ideal Audience Member your heart most wants to serve. Will you tell me about that person?" I asked her.

"Gosh, I don't know," she said. "This is so hard. I know I'm supposed to niche and I know that this is supposed to be good for business, but I really do believe that everyone needs this."

If you try to talk to everyone, you will miss the chance to powerfully impact *anyone*.

If you have similar resistance to narrowing down your audience, it is based on completely founded beliefs. The truth is, pretty much everyone should know these things:

- What we eat affects every aspect of our lives.
- Your thoughts create your reality.
- High stress will ruin our health.
- Toxins in personal care products like shampoo and sunscreen increase our risk for cancer.
- You don't have to be miserable at work.
- Building muscle will dramatically increase your health and wellness.
- Your taxes don't have to be torturous.
- Kids need to move their bodies all day to be at optimum health and learning capacity.
- Insert your message here.

And yet, it matters immensely to whom we are saying these things, because the message that will reach one particular audience is different than the message that will reach another audience on the same topic.

YOUR REFINED ROOFTOP MESSAGE

| Your Rooftop Message | **+** | Focus On Specific Ideal Audience | **=** | Refined Rooftop Message |

It's easiest to understand the power of getting clear on your audience by reviewing some examples. Let me share some Rooftop Messages from the previous list of examples with different audiences.

General Rooftop Message: **"What we eat affects every aspect of our lives."**

Audience: Mothers of Young Children

Refined Rooftop Message: "Listen to me, mamas. I know you want to take amazing care of your babies. I also know that you are exhausted and there's never enough time in a day. I want you to know that you can feed your kids food they will enjoy that is healthy, that will help them thrive every day."

Audience: Athletes

Refined Rooftop Message: "Listen to me, athletes. I know that you work hard to play at the highest levels in your game, and I know that you want to take amazing care of your body. I also know that the information out there is very confusing about the right foods to eat for endurance, for strength, and for clarity of mind. I want you to know that there is a way to feed your body, and your athletic drive, every day in a way that is simple and efficient so that you can keep playing your sport at the level that you want to play."

Audience: College Students in Their First Year of School

Refined Rooftop Message: "Listen to me, college students. It is so exciting to finally be out from under the constant watch of your parents. I get that. In fact, I remember that. But here's the thing: What you put in your body has a direct impact on your ability to learn and perform in your classes, to stay up late and have an awesome time with your friends, and to do all of the other exciting adventuring on weekends that I know you want to do. So what you put into your body throughout your day can either make you feel awesome and excited about this new adventure at school, or it can make you feel miserable and interfere with your ability to be successful. Let me teach you how to eat so that you can feel awesome."

General Rooftop Message: "Your taxes don't have to be torturous."

Audience: Business Owners

Refined Rooftop Message: "Listen to me, business owners. I know that taxes are boring and feel like the last thing that you want to spend your time on. You are already wearing so many hats in your business. I know that taxes can feel complex, and like there's so much you need to remember and know in order to get this right. But here's what I want you to know: It's actually simpler than you think. There are only three things you really need to pay attention to in your business to do your taxes correctly as a business owner. Let me tell you what those are."

Audience: Inheritors of Large Sums of Money

Refined Rooftop Message: "Listen to me, inheritors. The mix of emotions that you are likely feeling right now can be very confusing. The sadness of losing someone who likely mattered a lot to you combined with the very real and understandable excitement of having a lot of money flow into your life can be overwhelming. It can also feel like a tremendous responsibility to "do right by" the money that has come your way. In addition, you are now responsible for a much more complex tax situation, or so you've heard. But I want you to know that your taxes don't have to be torturous, and that you can, in fact, enjoy your inheritance, the process of doing good with it, living out some dreams through it, and also get your taxes done right in a reasonable period of time. Let me show you how."

Audience: People Who Invest in Real Estate

Refined Rooftop Message: "Listen to me, real estate investors. I know that nobody wants to do taxes, right? But especially when you own multiple properties that may be in different places or have different zoning, or cover a large variety of investment situations, taxes can feel overwhelming and daunting. But when it comes to handling your real estate taxes, there are only three things you need to pay attention to. Let me tell you what those three things are so you can get taxes off your plate and go back to caring for and enjoying the fruits of all your labor from all your real estate investments."

General Rooftop Message: "Your thoughts create your reality."

Audience: Teenagers

Refined Rooftop Message: "Listen to me, teenagers. I know that it feels like there are so many decisions to make, that it's impossible not to make a mistake. You are in the tricky spot of enough life experience to know that things often don't go the way we plan, yet not quite enough experience to feel confident in making big decisions. It can be overwhelming and scary. But here's what I want you to know: you have more control over how your life feels than you think. So much of what happens in your world starts with your own thoughts. The awesome news is, you are the most important one who manages and works with your thoughts, which means you can be thinking thoughts that make life feel so much greater than you imagine."

Audience: Salespeople

Refined Rooftop Message: "Listen to me, salespeople. I know that picking up that phone can feel scary, especially if you've had a string of bad experiences on sales calls. No one likes being rejected. But here's what I want you to know: your success has so little to do with what happens on any of those particular calls. So much of that is out of your control. But here's what is in your control: the way you think about those sales calls. Your thoughts are actually the biggest variable in your reality. When you learn to choose thoughts that support your success, you will see a dramatic increase in your sales—and have so much more fun at work, too!"

Audience: Spiritual Conference Attendees

Refined Rooftop Message: "Listen to me, spiritual people. I know that you've heard so much about how your thoughts create your reality. There's a good chance that you already buy into this idea, as a matter of fact. But here's what I want you to know: there is a big difference between knowing your thoughts create your reality and actually practicing the thought work that dramatically improves your experience of your life. This is the opportunity I want to share with you today."

General Rooftop Message: **"Building muscle will dramatically increase your health and wellness."**

Audience: Older People at a Retirement Home

Refined Rooftop Message: "Listen to me, retirement home residents. I can just imagine how frustrating it is to not be able to do some of the things you used to be able to do physically. I hear it from my clients all the time. It feels like this is just one of those difficult aspects of aging. But here's what I want you to know: you can feel dramatically better—physically stronger and more vital than you can imagine right now—if you start a muscle-building exercise program today. There is a way to safely increase your health and wellness while actually enjoying your workout with friends who live right alongside you at your home."

Audience: Corporate Executives

Refined Rooftop Message: "Listen to me, corporate executives. I know it feels like you have no time to do the basics of taking care of yourself, much less enacting a muscle-building program. There are already more demands on your time and attention than you can possibly respond to. But here's what I want you to know: a simple, ten-minute-per-day muscle-building program will give you back at least three times that amount of time in increased energy and focus. You will be amazed at the impact it has on your life at work and beyond."

Audience: New Parents

Refined Rooftop Message: "Listen to me, new parents. I know that you had no idea what you were signing up for with this whole parenting thing. The interrupted sleep, the total loss of time to yourself (wonderful as your new baby is!) and the struggle to focus like you did before you started this parenting adventure is mind-blowing, really. But here's what I want you to know: you don't need a complicated workout routine to start taking care of your body again. A simple ten-minute-per-day muscle-building program will dramatically increase your ability to focus and feel great physically. You will be amazed at the impact it has on your life as a parent and beyond."

IF YOU TRY TO REACH EVERYONE, YOU'LL CAPTIVATE NO ONE

These examples illustrate how the way you communicate a message changes quite a bit depending on your audience. Now, if you were trying to speak to all these different kinds of audiences at once, it would require that you speak in a much more general way.

The message designed to reach "everyone" may sound something like this:

"Listen to me, beautiful people. I know taxes are no fun. Nobody wants to do their taxes. But it doesn't have to be as hard as you think. Whatever your situation is, there is a simpler way to approach your taxes, and we can probably decrease your tax bill. I want to help you get to that place, so let's talk."

As you can see, even with a heartfelt desire to help, the language necessary to reach out to all those people is inherently less compelling. You can't show them that you understand their unique circumstances simply because there is such variety in circumstances across all people. When you try not to turn anyone off by being too specific, you will end up saying something that isn't meaningful or compelling to anyone.

In Chapter 6 we will dive more deeply into how to get to know your audience in way that allows you to speak with them with such clarity and resonance. What's important now is that you understand the power of clarifying your Rooftop Message into one that will delight your ideal audience.

Chapter Four

YOUR THOUGHT LEADERSHIP STAND

Quick—say out loud Oprah's core message. Now, how about Tony Robbins—what is the central stand he takes in his speaking and work overall? Let's do one more: What does Sheryl Sandberg take a stand for in her thought leadership? Think of one of your favorite thought leaders and take a turn at articulating their stand—the message at the center of their work.

See how quickly and clearly you can articulate the message at the center of these well-known thought leaders' work? That's what you want for your own thought leadership stand.

Your Thought Leadership Stand is a succinct, one- to two-sentence version of your Refined Rooftop Message. It's the description of your thought leadership contribution that is compelling and simple so it's easy for anyone to share your Thought Leadership Stand with others. This makes it easier for you to talk about your speaking. It also makes it a whole lot easier for anyone you know to promote you as a speaker to others.

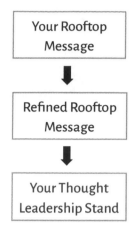

When your Thought Leadership Stand is articulated powerfully and in a compelling way, it will light up the meeting organizers and audiences who it is meant to serve. It makes it unwaveringly clear both what you solve with your speaking and the types of audiences you serve.

The most popular speakers in our world right now have strong and clear thought leadership stands. You see this all the time at conferences and other events. The same people are invited to speak on particular themes because they have taken a consistent stand for that message and those audiences. Here are some current examples of thought leaders who are taking a stand for a message with a particular audience:

Thought Leader	Thought Leadership Stand	Audience
Brené Brown	Vulnerability and courage are the path to living a wholehearted life.	People into personal development
Tara Mohr	When women play bigger, our whole world is served.	Women with dreams of doing bigger things in their life
Simon Sinek	Every meaningful successful pursuit has a clear and meaningful why at the center. Get yours.	People who want to build businesses or do other cool things
Susan Cain	When we understand and engage introverts better, our world will be a better place and we will all enjoy life together more.	Introverts and those who want to understand themselves and others
Shawn Achor	We can choose to be happier, and we should.	Corporate and business people who care about success and feeling good

The primary reason that these thought leaders are invited to speak on the most exciting stages in their industries is that they are recognized as the "go-to" person in their topic area. They didn't start there. They got there by starting with a message that matters, designed for a specific audience, and then consistently taking a stand for that message.

START WHERE YOU ARE RIGHT NOW

To become a go-to speaker in your industry, you start where you are right now, with the audiences you have available to you.

Begin to serve immediately. It's a wonderful time to test ideas and see how your ideas serve and shift. Transformational Thought Leadership is not about being "famous," though that may happen within your industry or even in the greater world. It's about *being of service*. We start from exactly where we are and begin to serve in the best way we can right now.

Transformational thought leadership is not about being "famous." It's about *being of service*.

CRAFTING YOUR THOUGHT LEADERSHIP STAND

I'm sure you have a handle on the concept of a Thought Leadership Stand at this point. Now is the time for you to turn that understanding into your very own compelling Thought Leadership Stand.

Here are some examples of Thought Leadership Stands to inspire you as you craft your own:

Enjoy a satisfying career, soak up time with your kids and play more your way.

Feel vibrant, strong and peaceful in your body—even when life is really busy.

Make your workouts your playtime and mealtime a nutritious family delight.

Lead your team with passion and focus and still enjoy life at work and home.

You can have a great relationship with your highly-sensitive teen.

Create a team of high-performers without stealing their life—or yours—outside of work.

Your Thought Leadership Stand is the stand you will take going forward with your thought leadership career. It will be at the center of your Rooftop Message Talk as well as all other ways you share your message.

EXERCISE: DECLARE YOUR THOUGHT LEADERSHIP STAND

Using your Rooftop Message and those you are meant to serve as a foundation of your statement, declare your Thought Leadership Stand using the guide below. Write your Thought Leadership Stand in your journal and mark the page. You will refer back to that journal page often.

I _____ [your name] take a stand for _____

[your ideal audience] that _____

_____ [your message].

Section Two

COMMIT TO SERVE

through

YOUR THOUGHT
LEADERSHIP STAND

Chapter Five

INTRODUCTION TO THE 5 C'S OF TRANSFORMATIONAL THOUGHT LEADERSHIP

*A*bout six years ago I had a poignant moment in my business that lead to a dramatic change in the way I understand and work with my thought leadership clients. I had just read an email from a client who was questioning everything about the talk she had just spent weeks crafting and refining. She was considering scrapping it all and starting over, wondering if all of this work she was doing was ridiculous, and that maybe she should just focus on her children and family for a while.

This conversation was so familiar to me that I felt my heart sink like a heavy rock in a glass of water. Why was this happening so often? Why were so many of my clients starting out with such passion and conviction, and then just when it was GO time, they would backpedal and decide that maybe it wasn't the right time, or they weren't the right person?

And my own deepest secret of all: *Why did I find myself asking these same questions of my own work far too often?*

I took my frustration out on a walk with my dogs. On this walk, I asked myself these questions: *What is the difference between those clients who had excelled in our work together and changed lives in a big and meaningful way with their message, and the far too many who quietly tucked away their*

45

beautifully-crafted talk in a bedside table drawer? What do those who are successful with their message have that the others do not?

What happened next is one of those almost spiritual experiences I've heard others describe but had never had for myself—until then. Within fifteen minutes of walking and talking, this entire model came to me. Yes, even all of the words starting with "C."

When I got home, I wrote out the model on a large flip chart paper on my wall. I held it up against client name after client name. Then, I held it up against all my favorite well-known transformational speakers and authors—awesome voices for good in our world—and found it to be consistently true: these are the characteristics of the most influential, heart-centered, transformational thought leaders. What's cool is that this also serves as a guide for you, if you want to make a meaningful difference through your own transformational thought leadership.

I immediately began working with clients around these characteristics and the results were exciting. When a client came to me struggling, I assessed which characteristic or behavior was lacking in their work. We zeroed in on that characteristic or behavior and their path to thought leadership opened up. They were feeling stuck—often for years—and this feeling began to gently loosen. Of course, it took work and a commitment to create new habits and patterns around these characteristics and behaviors, but referring to this model made it so much clearer how to stay on track.

THE FIVE C'S OF TRANSFORMATIONAL THOUGHT LEADERSHIP

Here are The Five C's of Transformational Thought Leadership that came to me on that walk in the woods:

1. Clarity
2. Commitment
3. Confidence
4. Caring
5. Charisma (natural)

This model acts as a valuable diagnostic tool, as well a clear guide for action to resolve any feelings of being stuck that you may be experiencing on your speaking and thought leadership path. The next five chapters cover each of these characteristics in more depth.

As you read through each of the chapters, ask yourself: How am I doing with this characteristic? How strong am I in this area? Each section has accompanying exercises you can use to address areas you need strengthened.

It's a fascinating thing to be called to serve as a speaker and thought leader. It can feel lonely and full of self-doubt at times because it's an audacious and courageous path. There's a good chance that you are not surrounded by people in your life who feel this same call, which may leave you wondering if you are being self-aggrandizing or otherwise "crazy" (many of us are called that, either quite directly or we can just feel it from those around us).

And yet here's what I know for sure: if the call beckons, it's your sign. You are meant to do this. While you may feel alone among family and friends, know that you are absolutely not alone in the greater world. You are a part of a magnificent group of mission-driven leaders who are committed to being a force for good in our world. And I for one am honored to be on this journey right alongside you.

If the call beckons, it's your sign. You are meant to do this.

These 5 Cs are a clear and focused way to turn away from thoughts of self-doubt and uncertainty and simply take one step after the other into service through that call you feel. And when you need it, Chapter 15 is full of ideas for how to move through fear to keep taking your courageous and life-changing steps forward.

The next five chapters cover each of the 5 C's in detail. The goal is to give you a deep understanding of how each characteristic looks and feels in your thought leadership as well as tools to help you embolden those characteristics that need strengthening.

Before we dive into the details of each of the characteristics, I want to introduce you to one of my long-time clients who embodies the 5 C's beautifully, and enjoys the benefits of having established herself as a thought leader in her industry.

Dina is a designer who specializes in elementary schools as part of an architecture team. We met about six years ago when she was at the tail end of a ground-breaking research project. In this project, she was part of a multi-disciplinary team with public health experts, school administrators, and university researchers. The team came together to create an academic study around kids and wellness related to the built environment using a real upcoming school build project.

The project was so innovative and exciting that Dina and the team were invited to present their experience at some of the most respected conferences in their industries. In fact, six years later, Dina and her team still deliver presentations with ideas from this project as well as many new insights that have arisen after that initial project was completed.

If we use Dina as an example, we can see how the 5 C's of Transformational Thought Leadership play out in real life action.

THE 5 C'S OF TRANSFORMATIONAL THOUGHT LEADERSHIP IN ACTION

Clarity: Dina and her team take a stand for the power of the built environment to influence kids' behavior and choices, especially as they relate to wellness and learning. Her ideal audience is educators, school administrators, architects and others who directly impact decisions made around designing and building spaces for kids.

Commitment: Dina has spoken at many conferences, large and small, all over the world for the past six years. She writes for industry publications, too. She is devoted to helping make schools a place for kids to thrive in health and learning.

Confidence (competence + conviction): Dina shares her experience with great competence and conviction when she speaks. There is no doubt in a listener's mind as to whether Dina cares deeply about the impact her work makes in the lives of others, nor whether she knows what she's talking about. In fact, at times my greatest challenge as her coach is helping her translate her deep expertise into terms that broader audiences will understand, not uncommon when working with experts.

Caring: The conviction Dina expresses comes from a very real connection with the difference her work makes in the lives of the kids who attend the schools she builds. You can hear this in the stories she tells about the first day of a new school opening and watching the kids leap into and enjoy the new space she was lucky to be a part of creating.

Charisma (Natural): As I said earlier, Dina has extensive expertise—and the vocabulary to go with it. She's an academic at heart. What I know from my years as a speaking coach is that the most engaging style of speaking is your most natural style. That said, you must connect with and serve your audience above all else. Dina works hard to weave her natural, intellectual style of speaking with captivatingly warm stories about the kids she meets so that her audiences get the best of her while also feeling connected and served by her content.

Wouldn't it be so fun to write up one of these 5 C's of Transformational Thought Leadership assessments about your own speaking?! After you work through the next five chapters, you should be able to do just that.

For now, you can take the assessment quiz on the book resources website page and learn which of the 5 C's will most embolden your thought leadership goals. You can access the book resources page at **beyondapplausebook.com/resources**.

In the next five chapters, you will learn how each of these characteristics plays out in Transformational Thought Leadership as well as tools to strengthen any of the Cs that need support in your own leadership speaking.

Chapter Six

CLARITY

"**I** want people to know that they can do anything they want to, if they just put their minds to it and believe it's possible," said this big-hearted potential client during our first strategy call.

"What a beautiful message," I said. "To whom do you want to say this—and what kinds of things does he or she want that they are struggling to have right now?"

"Oh, it doesn't matter! That's the thing. I believe everyone can create the life they dream of having. That's what's so amazing about the work I get to do! I've seen it change so many people's lives under so many different circumstances."

Ah, the ever-elusive, yet oh-so-essential clarity! The fact is, clarity is magic for confidence, conviction, and action—all of which are vital to your commitment to becoming a transformational thought leader. And yet, the kind of clarity you need to inspire the greatest impact in the lives of those you serve requires a kind of focus and specificity that can be difficult for a mission-driven, heart-centered person. It requires a commitment to serving a specific audience with a crystal clear message that matters deeply for them.

Clarity is probably the most sought-after and the most elusive experience for every messenger, speaker, and thought leader I've ever worked with. I, too, have experienced a great deal of confusion in this realm, in the early days of my business. It's normal to be unsure of exactly what to take a stand for when first deciding to step into thought leadership, because there is still so much to be learned about *how* to take a stand.

It doesn't work to pretend to have clarity (I've tried that—just as most of us have). It is important to do the work to land on the message you want to take a stand for, the one that lives at the heart of the commitment to serve others. This is where the work you did on your Rooftop Message and your Thought Leadership Stand comes in. That stand you take is at the heart of Clarity. Note: sometimes clarity is confused with a desire for certainty. Please don't look for certainty, you won't find it.

The good news is, clarity can be broken down into elements that together will lead you to a stronger sense of direction and ability to take positive action.

The most important elements of clarity on your thought leadership path are:

- Your message—also known as, Your Thought Leadership Stand.
- Who you serve.
- The difference you want to make.

CLARITY OF YOUR MESSAGE: YOUR THOUGHT LEADERSHIP STAND

For the first six years in my business, most of my clients came to me because they wanted clarity of their message. They had a general idea of what they wanted to say, but they didn't feel confident in the way they were saying it, nor how it was distinctive from others who had a similar message. This was very satisfying work because the levity and delight I got to experience with my clients after they got clear on their message was just awesome.

Clarity of your message is important for two reasons: it guides you in your speaking and thought leadership, and it helps the audience experience the transformation they are seeking.

Without a focused and clear message, speakers end up disappearing into the mass of all possible speakers for events in a general category. This was the case for Karen when we first started working together. A powerhouse woman with an impressive background, Karen has been called on to speak on a variety of topics because she's an engaging communicator with great stories to tell. This approach worked while she was just speaking on the side, as a fun but non-essential part of her work. But when Karen decided to get serious about taking her place as a thought leader in her industry, the first thing she needed to do was get crystal clear on her Thought Leadership Stand and who she serves. Doing that work was magic for her goals as a speaker. She updated her speaker bio and speaking topics and began reaching out to conferences where her Ideal Audience Members were spending their time. Not only did she begin getting invitations to speak at some of the most respected conferences in her industry, but she was also contacted by multiple high-end magazines that wanted to quote her in upcoming articles.

When your message is powerful and clear, as with a Thought Leadership Stand, you are top of mind in your topic area when a conference organizer is looking for speakers. Everyone who knows you knows when to refer you. This gives you a huge network of advocates for your speaking career.

EXERCISE: REVISIT YOUR THOUGHT LEADERSHIP STAND

In the previous chapter, you did the good deep work of crafting your Thought Leadership Stand. You don't need to do that work again. Just go back to your journal now and revisit the stand you wrote. As you work through the following exercises about whom you serve, you will likely have new insights that you will also want to integrate. Make updates to Your Stand as needed after working through each of these exercises.

CLARITY ABOUT WHOM YOU SERVE

Karen, from the story above, was clear from the beginning who she serves: passionate women who want to change the world. She didn't need any more clarity on this. She just needed to get clear on the particular stand she wanted to take with and for those women.

Often, though, the opposite is true. Clients will come to me with a pretty good idea of what they want to say but they just can't commit to a specific audience to serve. This is understandable because the fact is that their message can serve so many people. There are a whole lot of people in our world who would be well-served to know about nutrition, time management, how to make more sales, how to have difficult conversations, and so many other valuable messages.

However, you can't serve your audience in a way that changes their lives if you can't speak their language specifically. There is no better way to connect with your audience than to say out loud the same thoughts they are saying to themselves that they think no one else understands. We can only do this when we have a very specific audience and we get to know them intimately.

EXERCISE: GETTING INTIMATELY CONNECTED WITH YOUR IDEAL AUDIENCE MEMBER

A great way to decide on your Ideal Audience Member is to think of one person you know who really needs this message. Maybe it's a friend or family member, or maybe it's a client who came to you for this very reason and her life has been dramatically changed by your work together. If you have experienced the same transformation yourself that you are offering to your audience, it may even make sense to use yourself, before your learning and growth, as your Ideal Audience Member. (Note: if you use yourself, remember to refer only to your thoughts, ideas, and experiences *before* your transformation. You have language, knowledge, and experiences now that you didn't have then. Don't get them confused.)

As you think about your Ideal Audience Member, hold this person in your mind and heart as you answer the following questions. Grab your journal to record your answers.

What is this person struggling with most that you can solve? Write that out in their words.

What does s/he desperately wish for? What solution would light them up and make them very happy?

What does s/he think is the problem that's causing their struggle? (Note that I'm not asking what you think is the problem. What do they think is the problem?)

What does it feel like for this person inside this struggle? Use feeling words here.

What does s/he want to feel instead of these difficult or uncomfortable feelings s/he's feeling now?

What else do you know about your Ideal Audience Member—struggles, dreams, "reasons" the struggle isn't yet resolved?

It's not all about struggle. This person enjoys hobbies, life, and socializing, too. Where does s/he like to go for fun and to enjoy the company of others?

The more intimately you understand your Ideal Audience Member, the more powerfully you can speak to that person in your thought leadership talk.

EXERCISE: DRAW YOUR IDEAL AUDIENCE MEMBER

This exercise is the most fun and useful Ideal Audience Member exercise of all. (By the way, it also works well as an Ideal Client Exercise, which, for many thought leaders who are attracting clients through speaking, is an exercise about essentially the same person.) My clients love it and are delighted with the unexpected insights they gain. I am confident that will happen for you as well.

Directions:

1. Set aside 30 minutes to an hour.
2. Hang a large sheet of paper on your wall. (I like the sticky ones that have adhesive on them, but you can use any kind of paper and tape. If you don't have large paper, a regular 8.5" x 11" or legal size sheet will do but you're going to need a lot of room to write a lot of words, so the bigger the piece of paper, the better.)
3. Grab as many colored markers as you can find.
4. Draw a totally imperfect picture of your ideal client. Give them hair and eye color. Think about their clothing, too. It doesn't have to be perfect, and it may or may not matter what they are wearing, but that depends on your Ideal Audience Member. Also include what they are holding in their hands. (Coffee cup all day long? Cell phone to ear? Briefcase, diaper bag, gym bag, hanging from the crook of the elbow?)
5. Add context to the drawing. What's in the room with this person (a clock because s/he's always watching the time? A desk full of papers? Stacks of laundry on the back of the couch?)
6. Now here's the most important part: Draw thought bubbles above this person's head. Fill in those bubbles with their thoughts, in their words. Include all of their thoughts—especially those secret ones they think one one else ever thinks or knows that they think to themselves. Some of the common thoughts that I see across many Ideal Audience Members are: "Am I ever going to figure this out?" "What

the hell is wrong with me?" "I'm exhausted!" "Why am I so miserable?" Be sure to include very specific thoughts about the struggle she is experiencing as well.

Perfectionist note: This is not about your drawing skills! This may be especially hard for you if you are an artist and are used to drawing well. (You'll see that I don't have this problem in the example on the book resources page.) This exercise is most effective if you just go for it—stick figure or quick sketch drawing. It's her thoughts that matter—spend the most time there. Her surroundings and context overall are important, too, so go deep in those areas, but not by making the desk in the background look like a French Provincial number from the early 1800s.

You aren't going to share this exercise with anyone else. It's only meant to be a visual reminder of exactly who you are serving with your message and what this person really needs and wants, as well as the unique struggles around getting there.

The most important thing that you can do as a thought leader and speaker is understand who you serve and what they're struggling with—and speak to that struggle with deep resonance and care. This is a valuable tool to keep you steeped in that connection with your Ideal Audience Member so that when you offer solutions, you know that you're offering solutions to the things that are the most important and the most compelling for your Ideal Audience Member.

The most important thing that you can do as a Thought Leader and speaker is understand who you serve and what they're struggling with—and speak to that struggle with deep resonance and care.

CLARITY ABOUT THE DIFFERENCE YOU WANT TO MAKE

Grace wants to inspire hundreds of women from the stage, like a female version of Tony Robbins. Remember how clearly she stated that in our conversation outside her office at the start of this book? This kind of clarity about the impact you want to make is essential to your thought leadership path.

Maybe you're like Grace and you want to speak on large stages to audiences in the thousands. You may have a goal that speaking will be your primary source of income. Knowing what you want to create for yourself and the world through your thought leadership is an essential foundation for a satisfying thought leadership career.

Your visions for the difference you make may be less about large stages, and more about deep impact and transformation. Your thought leadership goals may be about speaking at smaller conferences and workshops, and getting more concentrated time with the people in attendance.

If you lead your organization, your goals for thought leadership speaking may be about inspiring and serving your teams to reach overall business and culture goals in your organization. Your goal may be to bring in as much donor money as possible to your non-profit.

We can't ignore one of the most exciting outcomes of high-impact speaking for those who want to attract awesome clients. Speaking is the most powerful way I know of to attract clients you love. For the right people in the room, your talk is exactly what they need to decrease the uncertainty of what it would be like to work with you and compel them to work with you on their full transformation.

EXERCISE: VISIONING THE DIFFERENCE YOU MAKE

This exercise will help you get clear on the difference you really want to make with your thought leadership. From this exercise, you will be able to create goals, strategies and tactics that help ensure that you make the meaningful impact you want to make in the world.

Set aside 15 to 20 minutes for this exercise. Get comfortable in a place where you have privacy and won't be interrupted. (If you'd like to follow a recorded version of this visualization, you will find one on our book resources page at **beyondapplausebook.com/resources**)

Sit comfortably in a chair or on the floor, closing your eyes when you feel ready.

Start by relaxing each part of your body, starting at your toes and moving up slowly along your legs, hips, waist, back and tummy, chest, shoulder blades, shoulders, neck...all the way up your face and back of your neck to the very top of your head. Consciously invite every part of you to relax and let go.

When you are ready, move your attention to the spot inside your head behind your eyes. You are going to play a movie here, so imagine a screen or area there where you can watch the scenes.

The first scene is you lying in your bed, just starting to wake from a great night's sleep. The date is two years out from now, and life is feeling really good for you in this scene. The decisions you've made and the work you've done have lead to a life that feels great to you. Pay special attention to the details around you as you wake up.

What do you notice about the room you are in? Furniture and bedding—what colors do you see and what kind of materials? Do the walls have artwork? Is there a window? Notice all of these details of the room.

Now you are walking out of the bedroom and starting your day. Where are you going first? Are you having breakfast with someone? If so, who—and what do you talk about over breakfast?

It's time for your first meeting of the day. Who is it with and what is the meeting about? Where does this meeting happen?

Take time to notice what you are wearing on this lovely day in your great life two years from now. What colors and style of clothing? Notice your shoes.

After your meeting, you are traveling back to your office or wherever you work when you get a phone call. You pull over to a safe spot to take this phone call. You are so glad you did because this person has some extremely exciting news for you. What is the news? Why does it matter so much to you?

Take yourself through the next few hours of the day. Go to your office. Notice what it looks like and who is there.

Pay special attention to what you are doing while you are working.

Are you preparing a talk—and if so, where will that talk be delivered? And what is the title of that talk?

Are you writing articles—and if so, for what publications?

Maybe you are working with clients or some other kind of projects— notice as many details as you can.

Let the scene play out on the screen behind your eyes in an easy way.

Notice what you do in the evening and as your day turns to night.

When you have experienced a full day on the movie screen in your mind, walk yourself back to your bedroom, pull back the covers and climb back into bed.

But don't open your eyes yet...

It is now ten years out and you are again waking up in your bed, into an even more awesome life where you are contributing beyond your dreams.

Notice if it's the same bed or a new space or furniture and bedding. Just make note.

Then walk yourself through the same events as above, only this time they are happening ten years from now. Things are different in your life and in your work. What are those details?

Make notes of everything that comes to you. Don't judge whether it's useful of not, just notice.

And when your day is ready to close, walk yourself back to that cozy bed in your bedroom of ten years from now and go back to sleep.

When you are ready, open your eyes and answer these questions in your journal, one answer for each of the two phases of this visualization, two years out and ten years out:

What did you notice about your bedroom, home and life?

What was that first meeting you had about and who was it with?

The phone call while you were driving—who was it and what was the news?

The projects you were working on, what were they?

If you were crafting a talk or writing an article, what was the title and content of those?

What did you do in the evening and then later in the night before bed?

What other details stood out that you want to capture? Just write them down.

What was different about the ten years from now visualization? Did you notice a difference in the way you felt? Were your projects different? Was your house or office different? Write down all of the details.

While this exercise may seem only slightly related to thought leadership, I have found it to be highly useful in my work with clients. Allowing your mind to reveal its dreams and ideas without too much direction leads to some of the most incredible insights. These insights can inform the goals you set for your impact as a thought leader. Here are some goals you might set for your thought leadership:

- Speak on a TEDx stage in the coming year to spread your message of hope far and wide.
- Raise $50,000 for your favorite cause through speaking to donors.

- Naturally attract 20 new clients this year through speaking gigs.
- Receive at least 80% of feedback forms expressing a significant positive shift in audience thinking about their struggle.
- Persuade 100 people to stop buying toxic cleaning products for their home (as measured by follow-up surveys).
- Speak on 15 stages for events full of ideal customers to build brand awareness and change their lives with your message and products.

Your goals may be significantly different than these, but the important thing is that you spend some time really determining what you want to create through your thought leadership and then build your talks and your strategy with those goals at the heart.

Chapter Seven

COMMITMENT

When I got home from my walk in the woods those years ago when the 5 C's of Transformational Thought Leadership came to me, I started to do some research. This brought about a profound "ah-ha" around my own commitment to my message and my work. I realized that this was the number one obstacle in the way of my own success. When I held my name up to those 5 C's and got to Commitment, in rushed the memories of all the times I took "sabbaticals" from my work. There were many periods when I "cut back on work" to focus on a remodel of our home, or care for our girls over summer break. While there is nothing inherently wrong with those choices, it was immediately clear to me that this lack of commitment to consistency in my thought leadership contribution was at the heart of my own struggle to make the difference I felt so called to make.

My story is not uncommon among women I work with who are mothers. Many of us who juggle businesses, motherhood, and leadership of home care can get overwhelmed by all there is to do. But mothers aren't the only ones who struggle with this.

I have worked with many clients who struggle with taking the concentrated time and energy necessary to get crystal clear on their message and then take consistent action to establish thought leadership. It feels like an exciting idea at the outset, but the payoff can be hard to keep in sight at times—especially while juggling so many other things at the same time. The path to becoming a recognized thought leader can be long and not-so-glamorous, especially in the early days. It takes a deep commitment to the long-game to make it work.

There is so much uncertainty, especially in the early stages of stepping into thought leadership. Aspiring thought leaders will speak once and then pull back for months, questioning whether they want to put themselves out there in such a public way. Or, they do one podcast interview and then never share it with their audience. Stepping into thought leadership with the intention to make a big impact is not for the faint of commitment.

Stepping into thought leadership with the intention to make a big impact is not for the faint of commitment.

The good news is that so much momentum is available on the other side of commitment. Many people simply don't realize that commitment is the issue. It's easy to think those "reasons" are the actual reasons, when they are really excuses to protect from the discomfort that is inherent in being visible and taking a stand for our ideas in a big way.

Of course, you can continue to use those "very good reasons" to avoid your greatest work and make the impact you feel compelled to make. It's a choice. But you don't get to do both. You can't be a known thought leader *and* hide from the spotlight; the two are mutually exclusive.

WHY COMMITMENT MATTERS ON THE PATH TO THOUGHT LEADERSHIP

I recently facilitated an interactive webinar on how to reach far and wide with your message through speaking. In this webinar, I introduced The 5 C's of Transformational Thought Leadership. While I received a number of comments and emails about each of the 5 C's, Commitment was by far the most frequent C that webinar attendees identified as their struggle. This was a linchpin insight for attendees of that webinar. Upon reflection, it was clear that while they were "working" on sharing their message, when they looked more honestly at their willingness to do what it takes to share their message, they were wavering regularly. And frankly, hiding much of the time.

It's easy to look and feel like you are working today, especially with social media. If I post something, aren't I stepping out into the arena?

Yes, in a way you are. However, we all know that there are as many ways to post on social media as there are green juice combinations.

Does what you are sharing speak meaningfully to the heart and soul of what your audience needs and wants? Most important: does it serve them in a way that matters?

These are the questions you need to be asking yourself.

One of the most fascinating truths I have found in working with founders of very successful and fast-growing companies and organizations is that at the heart of the work they are doing they have a sort of maniacal commitment and belief in their ability to share something that matters. Any wrench that gets thrown in the road along the way is simply something to resolve in order to realize their vision. It does not stop them—it compels them to do whatever it takes to move through that potential barrier.

Founders of very successful and fast-growing companies and organizations have a sort of maniacal commitment and belief in their ability to share something that matters.

It is crystal clear to me that this kind of commitment is the most essential difference between those who want to serve in a big way with their message but can't quite figure out how, and those who rise up with their booming voice for good, and make certain they serve no matter what. I'm going to assume you are ready to commit in full action. What does commitment in action look like?

First and foremost, it's about crafting and delivering your message—especially your transformational thought leadership talk (which I call Your Rooftop Message Talk) in a way that makes the greatest impact, which we talk about in more detail in Chapter 12. Then it's about sharing that message as far and wide as possible, which is discussed throughout Section Three of this book.

IT'S A DECISION TO COMMIT—AND THEN IT'S A VERB

Making a commitment to thought leadership is like committing to a relationship. You listen to your heart, and when it feels clear and right, make a decision. It's a declaration. "I'm doing this. I'm in it for the long haul. I'm committed to the journey to serve."

Like a love relationship, you need to be both committed and flexible. Your love relationship grows and changes, as does your thought leadership experience. The most important commitment you make in your thought leadership is to your audience. You commit to making a positive difference in their lives with your own stories, life lessons, and expertise. While clarity of your message is essential, it may very well evolve as you learn and grow in thought leadership.

"MESSAGE LEAPING" IS A COMMITMENT ISSUE

One of the things I see aspiring thought leaders struggle with is that they leap from message to message. Before they have a chance to really test one message out, then shift and grow their message and impact, they are dropping that message and moving to another. I did that very thing, too, in my early years in business. Some of that is a natural part of "trying on" your message. The key is, if you want to get on the best stages as a speaker, the event organizers need to know what you stand for so they know you are a perfect fit for their audience. That comes much more easily when you're seen as a "go-to" person for your message and for that particular audience. You need consistency of message, which comes from commitment.

YOUR COMMITMENT TO IMPACT

Part of commitment is impact, which means delivery excellence in your thought leadership, especially your speaking. Essentially this is about crafting a captivating, inspiring, and highly useful talk. A commitment to serving at the highest level also means sharing your best ideas, stories, and lessons learned through other media through which your audience takes in learning and inspiration. This means publishing articles, being interviewed on podcasts, and appearing online and on television shows, for example. If you are committed to being a recognized and sought-after speaker so you can serve from those awesome stages, then you are always looking for ways your work can serve your audience through multiple channels.

KNOW WHY BECOMING A SOUGHT-AFTER SPEAKER MATTERS TO YOU SO MUCH

Simon Sinck is a thought leader in the business world, and is the author of the book *Start with Why*. He has delivered many talks, TED-style and otherwise, on this topic. The heart of his message is this: *We must center our missions and our messages around our deepest "Why."* It is that "Why" that carries us through the ups and downs of tough roads. It's our connection with *why* we are doing what we are doing that keeps us going. And it is this very "Why" that makes the strongest connection with those we are meant to serve.

In my experience, when we hear this simple proclamation, "Start with Why" we instinctively feel the truth in it. But our understanding of our own "why" doesn't happen automatically. It requires inquiry and invitation. We need to take the time to ask ourselves the question, "Why does this matter so much to me?" You will find a story there—very likely, a story of transformation that is driving your desire to serve through this message.

EXERCISE: CONNECT WITH YOUR "WHY"

Let's take time now to get connected with your own why, and the story at the heart of your why. Grab your journal and answer the questions below without taking too much time to overanalyze each one. Let your thoughts flow easily.

Why does sharing this message as a speaker matter so much to you?

Why do you feel so strongly about making this difference?

What is the story at the heart of your why? What happened for you that drives your passion for this topic?

What will happen if you don't step into a thought leadership role? How will the lives of those you are meant to serve be impacted?

WHY DOES THIS MESSAGE MATTER SO MUCH TO YOUR IDEAL AUDIENCE MEMBER?

A few years into my business I went through a really hard time both in my work and in my personal life. I was working with a brilliant coach named Paula who was helping me prioritize as well as see the brighter picture through some shadowy days. One day, after a strategy session in which we put together a plan that was both exciting and scary to me, I said to her: "Paula, I just don't think I can do this. I just don't feel capable of making it happen." And she said to me, "That's okay, Michelle. I'll hold the belief for you that you ARE powerful. I can completely and fully see you taking action on this plan and making it happen. You just need to lean in and take the first step. From there, momentum flows. You don't even have to believe it yet. Just begin."

I played that conversation in my mind many times as I moved forward with that plan. I believed her and was able to use her belief to fuel my actions, however imperfect and slow-going they may have been. Paula was able to be so steadfast and certain in her belief in me, and committed to supporting my action because she was intimately connected with my "why." She knew that my reason for doing this work was heart-filled and deep.

What Paula did for me is the kind of commitment you want to be able to help your Ideal Audience Member hold. When you understand their deepest "why," you can become an advocate for that reason, even when that person feels too afraid or overwhelmed by what it takes to get to the other side of struggle.

EXERCISE: CONNECT WITH THE "WHY" OF YOUR IDEAL AUDIENCE MEMBER

In the previous chapter, you did some rich work on understanding your Ideal Audience Member. Refer back to those exercises to get reconnected with them. Then, grab your journal and answer these questions to help deepen your own commitment to your thought leadership:

What problem is my Ideal Audience Member experiencing right now that I can help them solve?

What are they experiencing in their lives right now as a result of this problem?

What is the "fallout" that results from not solving the problem?

What feeling words would they use to describe the struggle they are experiencing?

What thoughts are running through their minds as they tangle with this situation?

What are the current barriers to getting to the other side of their struggle?

What have they tried that has not worked to solve this problem?

After they experience your talk, how will their life change in a way that matters?

What feelings will they experience once they resolve this struggle once and for all?

EXERCISE: CREATE YOUR OWN COMMITMENT RITUAL

You've got your Rooftop Message, you know who you serve through that message and you are connected with why this transformation matters. This is the perfect time to make a commitment to the people you want to serve by creating a ritual around that commitment. This ritual serves as an anchor for your promise to serve. It's human nature to question yourself at times, and a physical emblem of your commitment plus a thoughtful activity can provide a reminder of that commitment. When you have moments of wavering, you can refer back to your ritual experience and associated item to remind yourself of the commitment you made, and why it matters to you.

Here are a few suggested rituals:

- **Purchase a special ring, bracelet, necklace, or other jewelry item.** This ritual has been rewarding and meaningful for both men and women. If you prefer more masculine jewelry, there are very cool copper bracelets and wood-beaded artisan necklaces (my husband,

Jim, has a whole collection of these he likes to wear) that are a great choice for this ritual. Choose a special place to declare your commitment, possibly with a trusted friend or coach to witness, and adorn yourself with the item after your declaration. Every time you wear that item, it will remind you of your commitment to those you are here to serve. I found a gorgeous artisan-designed ring that I wear especially when I want to feel deeply connected with my Ideal Audience Members all around the world.

- **Write your commitment in the form of a letter to your Ideal Audience Member on high-quality stationery.** Mail it to yourself or someone you want to help you hold this commitment.

- **Search out and find a piece of artwork that represents this commitment to your Ideal Audience Member.** Hang that artwork somewhere that will remind you every day of your commitment to bring your brilliance in this way. (I found mine in the form of a gorgeous, artist-rendered greeting card. With a simple store-bought frame, it doesn't have to cost a lot to do this.)

- **Create a custom T-shirt with a phrase or image that represents your Ideal Audience Member and the transformation you are committed to helping them realize.**

- **Buy a new pair of running shoes or yoga mat.** When you go out for a run or begin your yoga practice, spend a moment dedicating your session to your Ideal Audience Member. Hold their greatest expression in your heart throughout the session.

Chapter Eight

CONFIDENCE

*J*ennifer has been an executive coach since before the term "executive coach" had a definition. She rose in the ranks of leadership at her manufacturing company and then landed in HR as counsel and guide to leaders at every level on anything employee related. She has years of experience at virtually every level and in nearly every department in the organization. That's not all she has, though. She is also a certified executive coach and has multiple certificates in advanced coaches training. She was much loved in her corporate work and she is a respected coach now. Suffice to say, Jennifer is pretty awesome. It will come as no surprise that she also has an incredible number of stories, life lessons, and a great deal of expertise as a thought leader.

But Jennifer hasn't really stepped into thought leadership much at all. Despite some really deep work together crafting her inspiring thought leadership talk, she just can't seem to make the leap to step onto stages to share her message. Every time she decides she's going to get out there and offer to speak on bigger stages, she decides she's going to take one more class first to hone up her skills.

Jennifer struggles with confidence.

I notice that people tend to avoid the word confidence. I think it's because it feels vague and inaccessible, as if you either have it or you don't. I've heard people say that it's overused and misused. While this last point may be true, ignoring the value of confidence simply because others may be using it too often or incorrectly skips over an important variable in your success as a thought leader. Confidence is a critical element in both your sense of self as a thought leader, and in your audience's experience of you as a transformational thought leader.

WHY CONFIDENCE MATTERS

To trust—meaning to believe in the content and to take action on your ideas—your audiences must *experience* confidence from you. And to express confidence for your audience, you must feel a sense of confidence *within* yourself.

Confidence is a broad-reaching word. As such, it's hard to grab hold of any element to take action on it. Therefore, it's helpful to break the word confidence down into two element words. The fun thing is you get two more C-words out of this. I see confidence expressed most clearly through two elements:

When your competence is clear (you know what you're talking about and it shows), and you express your ideas with conviction (passion and clarity), your audiences experience you as confident. This experience of confidence for your audience is essential to your ability to make an impact.

THE ELEMENTS OF COMPETENCE

Competence is the ability to successfully serve with your expertise. For our purposes, there are two parts to competence. There is competence at sharing your thought leadership (being an engaging speaker, interviewee, writer) and there is subject-area competence, your actual expertise.

Breakdowns in confidence come in both areas of competence. The problem comes when you use a desire for more "competence" as a "good reason" to avoid stepping into thought leadership. You see this happening with Jennifer in the example at the beginning of this chapter. She says she wants to step into thought leadership and I know she means it. I can hear and feel her conviction. But she's struggling with her *belief* in her competence.

Notice I didn't say she's struggling with her actual competence—just her belief in her competence. This is another area where stealthy fear can get in your way, telling you that you aren't competent enough to serve. There will always be another course, certification or degree you can hang on your wall. You've got to know when you are competent enough to serve—and then get out there and start serving. This is where Jennifer was struggling.

Subject-Area Competence

Subject-area competence is your experience and skill in your own content area. As an energy healer, for example, this is your years of experience helping clients release energy blocks. It is also the Reiki and light healing certifications you have obtained during your time as a healer. As an executive coach, your subject-area competence may be a combination of your years working as a leader in organizations combined with your coach training and experience coaching others. This experience might be within one industry, or it might be a variety of industries, and your competence is strengthened by your broad experience across industries.

The greatest strength in your subject-area competence may come from the niche in which you have spent years working. For example, the deep understanding that comes from rising in the ranks of retail is impossible to replicate with a certification or other designed training. The same is true in most niche areas so be sure not to discount this element of your competence, if it applies.

The key with subject-area competence is to take a look at and recognize your unique experience and use that complete story to support your confidence as a thought leader.

The question you want to ask yourself around competence is: "Do I have the level of competence that I need to serve this audience well with my expertise, my stories, and my lessons learned?" Keys to note here are "level of competence... to serve this audience." An important part of working within your competence is simply about the audience you serve.

Let me give you an example.

Let's say you are a successful business coach who coaches other business owners to help them build freedom-focused businesses. These business owners keep their business model simple, create passive income flow and get to spend many hours a week away from work doing things they enjoy like surfing and traveling. This is the basis of your own message and expertise.

The important thing here is that when you choose your audience, you're choosing the audience that you can best serve with your message. You don't want to speak at a leadership conference full of bank and high-tech executives whose business cultures require long hours and a great deal of "face time" at work because you don't have competence (or interest) in those domains and types of business models.

As you assess your own competence, the first question to ask yourself is, do you really have a competence issue? And if so, is it simply a matter of shifting your audience to bring you back into alignment with your competence?

It may be that when you ask yourself this question, you realize that in order to serve the audience your heart is called to serve, you actually do need some more expertise in a certain area.

Let's say that you have been working as a health coach for a few years. As you've ventured down the health coaching path, you've had many clients come to you with more serious health issues than your training teaches you how to handle. You've been referring those clients to functional medicine doctors or specialists. With your current training and experience, you don't want to go to a functional medicine conference and speak on health and wellness. You just don't have the competence in treating the serious medical conditions the audience at that conference would demand.

You have a few choices in this scenario: 1) Don't go speak at that conference; or 2) If you're feeling the drive to move in that direction with your work, you could get functional medicine training.

Do what it takes to be competent with the message that you really want to share for the audience you are most compelled to serve.

> **Do what it takes to be competent with the message that you really want to share for the audience you are most compelled to serve.**

Special note here: you don't have to wait until you have that functional medicine training to serve. Start speaking at conferences that match your current competence while you are working through that training. By the time you complete your additional training, you will have substantially strengthened your thought leadership competence overall.

Thought Leadership Competence

Thought leadership competence is the ability to deliver a high-impact talk, speak clearly and with conviction on a podcast, or write an article or book that delights and serves the reader in a meaningful way. Beyond your expertise, it's also important that you are able to express your ideas in a way that moves and inspires people. This comes from thought leadership competence.

The good news here is, you're reading this book! So you're traveling up the thought leadership competence scale rapidly. As you clarify your thought leadership stand and make a plan for getting out there with your message in a bigger way, you may decide you want to get more support to increase your competency in thought leadership.

THE ELEMENTS OF CONVICTION

The second half of confidence is conviction. Conviction is the deep, visceral certainty that the problem you are solving matters enough to do whatever it takes to resolve it. It's the fire-in-the-belly desire to make a difference through your message and stories.

Conviction is the fire-in-the-belly desire to make a difference through your message and stories.

Conviction is an alchemical result of a combination of the 5 C's. It comes from crystal clarity about what you want to say, combined with confidence that your message will change lives and a deep caring about serving others with your message. This inspires a commitment within you to make the difference you are uniquely qualified to make through your stories and lessons learned. When you are deeply connected with the impact of your message in this way, expressing with conviction comes more naturally.

A strong connection with your own "why"—why this message matters to you—is the fastest path to your strongest conviction. Anytime you struggle to express your message with conviction, reading your own story of transformation or stories of transformation from those you've served is a reliable re-connection activity.

There's one more barrier to expressing conviction, even when you feel care and passion wholeheartedly. This pesky barrier can be tricky, too, often disguising itself as other things and making it difficult to diagnose and handle.

I'm talking about speaking anxiety. Speaking anxiety blocks your full expression. It can mask your conviction and stifle your passion, resulting in a kind of "flatline" or fumbling delivery, which makes you appear less competent and lacking in conviction.

How do you know if speaking anxiety is the culprit in a struggle to express conviction?

If you care deeply about your message and you feel committed to making a difference by sharing your expertise and stories but are struggling to express with strong conviction, then it is very likely that speaking anxiety is at play. This just means you'll want to spend some extra time with the strategies in Chapter 15. Speaking anxiety is manageable. You simply need to recognize it for what it is, and then take consistent action on transforming it.

EXERCISE: COMPETENCE & CONVICTION ASSESSMENT

Since confidence is essential to serving your audience, it's important that you know where you stand in your own sense of confidence. Use these questions to assess where you may want to concentrate on building your competence (or recognition of your competence) and your connection to conviction. Grab your journal and write out your answers in there.

My subject-area competence is in (name your area of expertise and, if relevant, the niche in which your experience is strongest)...

The audience I most want to serve is wishing for competent expertise from their speakers on these topics and/or solving these problems...

79

My subject-area expertise serves the audience I want to serve powerfully because...

As a speaker and thought leader, I have built competence through these trainings and experiences... (List out any speaking training or coaching, writing or publishing training or experience, and as many examples of places you've spoken and published in the areas of expertise you mention above.)

The reason I care so much about making a difference for others with my message is...

When I check in with myself honestly, I feel that my conviction around serving others with this message is at a (use 1-10 scale, where 1 = I'm just not feeling it, and 10 = off the charts). Given this, my next step is to... (Use the ideas from this chapter to make a plan for emboldening your conviction, such as "put practices in place to release speaking anxiety" or "revisit my 'why' story every day for the next thirty days."

When I think about my expressed conviction and the possible impact of speaking anxiety, I recognize that for me... (How does speaking anxiety impact the delivery of your message, if at all)?

I plan to take this action about any lingering speaking anxiety that may be interfering with my expressed conviction... (see Chapter 15 for ideas)

Chapter Nine

CARING

I was excited to talk with my client, Rochelle, after months between sessions. We had worked hard on refining her message and crafting a thought leadership talk she could offer to companies built on her many years of experience as a corporate executive. I excitedly asked, "What has happened since we last spoke? I know you had a few leads on speaking opportunities, what is the status with those?"

She sighed. Then paused.

"What's going on?" I asked.

"I haven't done anything with my talk. Not one single thing. I didn't even follow up on those leads."

I was stunned.

She had been so excited during our work together. She was ready to go for it, to finally say all the things she had wanted to say as an executive leader, but couldn't. She wanted to share inspiration and lessons learned with aspiring leaders to help them enjoy their work more than she had in her early leadership years.

But today I could hear none of that excitement.

"What happened?" I asked.

"I don't know. I walked away from our meeting so jazzed. But the next day, when I started practicing sharing this talk I felt totally flat. In fact, I felt kind of sick to my stomach. I just didn't want to do it. The truth is, I just don't want to speak to corporate audiences. I'm done with that part of my life."

What do you do if the message that you're sharing—or the audience you're speaking to—isn't at the heart of what you want to say or how you want to serve?

This happens more often than you may imagine. I rarely work with people who don't care at all about their message. This is because my clients are deliberately stepping into thought leadership out of a desire to serve in a way their hearts are called, not out of obligation or because it's in their job title. That said, even just the slightest misalignment in message or ideal audience can dramatically decrease passion and conviction for sharing that message.

It's an important question to ask: "Do I care deeply about this message and this audience? Is this the message and audience I feel *deeply called* to serve?"

If the answer is a resounding, "YES!" then carry on to the next chapter. Hooray for you!

If you feel a little twinge in your belly or a catch in your throat, please pay attention. Ask yourself what this physical message is trying to tell you. It is essential that you resolve any misalignment between your message and your audience. This may mean a shift to your message or a shift in your audience so that you can go out there and serve with passion and gusto with your message.

IT'S NOT THAT YOU DON'T CARE—IT'S THAT YOUR MESSAGE ISN'T QUITE RIGHT

Sometimes it's your successful business or career that trips you up. Your colleagues and clients know you for your current message so you feel you can't suddenly start taking a stand for a new message. You don't want to completely confuse your people and your thought leadership overall.

It could be that you started taking a stand for your current message during a different phase of your life. You've moved on from that phase, but you are well known for your expertise in that area. I've seen this happen with clients who help parents with infants, for example. They started with this message because they struggled with their own infants and found ways to ease the struggle. As their kids grow, their passion for the message they want to share shifts with new information and experience of new parenting phases. This is also what happened with Rochelle in the story at the start of this chapter. As her career path shifted, so did her desire to serve a different audience.

You may still feel completely passionate about your audience, but your message has changed. For example, you are committed to helping high-achieving engineers enjoy more success and satisfaction in their work and home life. Recently you have realized that even more important than life balance, which has been at the heart of your message, is the way these high-achieving engineers care for their energy through food and exercise.

Of course, it could be that your career has been all about a message you didn't choose consciously. You became the known thought leader in your area of expertise because you were really good and people saw that. You took a job, excelled at it, and were invited to share your expertise often. You enjoyed that for a long time but you are over that now. Maybe you are burned out on the message after many years taking a stand for it. You want to focus your energy and contribution in a different way going forward.

You may be noticing that these ideas I'm sharing about how to create stronger alignment with what you care about can come in conflict with the second "C" in the 5 C's of Transformational Thought Leadership, that is, Commitment. That chapter discussed the importance of making a commitment—especially to your audience.

And yet, as a mission-driven thought leader, alignment with your message and audience—and your mission overall—must be complete. I have seen over and over again the impossibility when a thought leader tries to take a stand that doesn't matter deeply to them. It just won't stick over time.

As a mission-driven thought leader, alignment with your message and audience must be complete.

This means you must make a shift to move into complete alignment with your message and audience. It's how you do this that matters most and that honors your commitment to your previous message and/or audience.

WAYS TO ALIGN YOUR THOUGHT LEADERSHIP WITH CARING

As we've covered, there are two elements to any message. There's the message that you're sharing, and there are the people you are serving through that message. Much of the time, you can find a rich connection with caring again when you focus on the people you are serving with the message.

Sometimes this just means getting reconnected with your Ideal Audience Member (for example through the Drawing Your Ideal Audience Member exercise in Chapter 6). A refinement of the message that serves this audience even better along with a few small shifts in the content of your message may be all you need. In the previous example about serving engineers, this does not require a whole revamp of message. It's still about helping engineers be successful and enjoy their jobs. You've simply enhanced the details of your message with even more useful information about food and movement.

My clients are coaches, wellness experts and leaders of conscious companies and non-profit organizations. They are people who support others in living their best, healthiest, most successful lives. While they care deeply about their audiences and making an impact, they can get burned out on serving because of the deeply personal nature of their work. If they haven't freshened up their own message and connection with their Ideal Audience Member, their speaking and thought leadership overall can lack energy and vibrancy over time. If you notice this lack of vibrancy happening for you, you may want to explore what might be going on for you. To do this, start by asking yourself these questions:

What have I learned in the last six months that has been an insight or an "a-ha"?

What client stories have made me feel excited, and what are the details of what happened for those clients?

Who have I met, read about, or heard speak who has reignited my passion for my message? How can I infuse that energy into my speaking?

What personal experiences have I had recently that have deepened my transformation and how can I integrate that information into my speaking and thought leadership overall?

This fresh dive into recent learning and experiences often revives your energy and your messaging, too. The richer connection with why your message matters and how it changes lives brings freshness to your conviction and stamina to your commitment.

Caring lives in your heart. This means you want to connect with your heart to check in on the strength of your caring. Asking and answering the questions shared in this chapter will help create the connection. However, nothing will inspire as deep a connection as sitting with, listening to, and serving your Ideal Audience Member directly. Your work with clients, your heart-to-heart conversations with audience members, friends, and anyone who struggles with the problems you help solve are the richest source of connection with your caring.

Nothing will inspire as deep a connection as sitting with, listening to, and serving your Ideal Audience Member directly.

Seek out opportunities to serve your Ideal Audience Members anywhere and as often as you can. Make a concerted effort to release preconceived ideas of what they need or may be experiencing and drop into your heart to listen and share with them. This isn't about your thought leadership in these moments, it's about the very special human connection that naturally arises when two people who share a similar experience come together in support.

EXERCISE: SEEK OUT AUTHENTIC HUMAN CONNECTION WITH IDEAL AUDIENCE MEMBERS

The goal with this exercise is to find as many ways to be in the company of your Ideal Audience Members as possible. Find ways to spend time with and enjoy them, to delight them and serve them, with as little "strategy" in mind as possible.

Here are some ideas for how to do this:

- Brainstorm places where your Ideal Audience Members hang out. Then, go hang out there with them. Enjoy the time with them.
- Make a list of everyone you know who fits your Ideal Audience Member description. Reach out to a few of them and invite them to coffee, lunch, or a movie. Enjoy the time with them.
- Call your favorite clients from the last few years. Invite them to a luncheon that you host so they can meet each other and make wonderful connections. Make the event as warm, inviting, and delicious as possible. Enjoy the time with them.

EXERCISE: IDEAL AUDIENCE MEMBER SACRED GETAWAY VISUALIZATION

This is a two-part exercise and doesn't have to take long. You may choose to make it longer simply because it feels so good as you experience it. Feel free to let it go as long as you like. It's a lovely and very useful way to spend some concentrated time in service of your impact in the world.

You are going to visit with your Ideal Audience Member in your Sacred Getaway. Have your journal handy to make notes at the end. This is a visualization exercise so you will want to find a comfortable quiet place where you'll have some privacy for at least ten minutes, maybe more if you are enjoying it.

When you are sitting comfortably in your quiet place (doesn't matter how—chair, floor, cushion), close your eyes. Allow your body to relax completely, starting at your toes and moving all the way up your legs, hips, spine and belly, chest and back...then up your neck. Let your shoulders drop and your face soften.

In your mind's eye, imagine you are walking in a beautiful place. The air feels perfect, and the surroundings are lovely. You are peaceful and excited because you are going to finally sit and connect with your Ideal Audience Member. It's been a long time since you two have sat together in person, and you've actually never had the chance to sit together for this purpose.

The purpose of this meeting is to get intimately connected with them. And it's also to deeply listen to your own internal messages, too. This is an honest conversation between two caring humans looking to serve one another.

You are walking along peacefully and getting closer to the building where you will sit with your Ideal Audience Member. It is coming into view. You are feeling even more excited because this feels like the perfect place for your meeting. Notice what it looks like and how you feel. Just notice. That's all.

You walk up to the door, which is open a bit. You walk in and there your Ideal Audience Member sits, with a big smile on their face. Notice your surroundings. Just make a note. You realize this beautiful space was perfectly designed for the two of you.

You walk over to your Ideal Audience Member and you give each other a warm hug. Then you sit down and begin talking. You catch up a little and then get to the heart of things. You ask them questions, and they ask you questions. You learn about each other, what they want and what you feel compelled to share with them. Your Ideal Audience Member shares with you what you are doing that is working so well for them—and also makes some suggestions. You ask them questions and make suggestions for them, too. It is a warm, caring exchange.

Stay in this conversation for as long as you like. Ask whatever you like. Listen to your Ideal Audience Member, and allow them to listen to you, too. Notice what you say to them. Notice what comes up in your body as you share with this person and listen to them.

When you are finished, give them a big thank you hug. Feel the genuine exchange of gratitude, going both ways. Then leave the space, walking back out the door you came in, and heading out the path that took you there earlier.

Open your eyes when you are ready and make notes in your journal about what you learned, especially about your heart connection with your Ideal Audience Member and the message. Did anything new come up? Any new shifts to the message or new ideas about your Ideal Audience Member? Note it all in your journal so that you can make the shifts that are necessary in your thought leadership that put you in the strongest alignment with your message and your Ideal Audience Member.

Chapter Ten

CHARISMA (NATURAL)

I walked into the large keynote talk about five minutes late, and the speaker was already on stage. Despite her small stature, her energy filled the large stage area. She was wearing high heels and a finely tailored suit, her blond hair easy in a cool bob cut. She was coming from stage right in the middle of a passionate story. She was talking about a time when her son asked her to put away all of her books on sex and intimacy because his friends were coming over and he didn't want them to see the books. In the throes of a research project, having her books strewn about was part of her work. She said to him something like, "Why would I put away books about sex and intimacy when our world is full of media about violence and hatred? Why would I not want you and your friends to know that there are many people who care about love and intimacy in our world?"

Her story was captivating, but the most compelling thing about watching Esther Perel speak was her energy and passion, with her arms moving out to her sides, walking straight toward us from the center of the stage and moving all the way to the other side of the stage to make great connection with the people on that side of the room.

There's nothing like watching a passionate, surrendered, fully-engaged speaker share their love and learning from the stage. And this is

Esther Perel's natural style of delivery. She is charismatic and dynamic in the ways you often think of in great speakers.

No question Esther Perel has "natural charisma."

Here's the important point: Esther's style of delivery is not the only way to be a charismatic speaker.

In fact, at the same conference, I was captivated watching Stella Paul of the organization World Pulse, whose delivery was much less physically active, but full of deep conviction in her voice and audience engagement. Her charisma was equally captivating—only different in the experience of it.

If you've seen Steve Jobs speak, you've experienced yet another kind of captivating engagement style fueled by a natural charisma that was all his own. Steve Jobs was known as one of the most compelling business speakers of all time, largely because of his casual delivery style mixed with an almost child-like delight at the subject of his talks—his very own Apple products. Most fascinating is the fact that Jobs' "causal" speaking style is the result of many, many hours of practice and refinement. Steve Jobs was known for his relentless commitment to captivating speaking that leaves the audience feeling like the whole presentation was "off the cuff."

Steve Jobs had charisma, no doubt, but it wasn't because he was born expressing himself that way. In fact, I like to think of charisma in an entirely different way.

WHAT IS CHARISMA, REALLY?

While we often think of charisma as something that people "have," I find it more useful to think of it as something people experience in others. This distance allows us to see charisma as a thing to be engaged or activated within you.

In the book *The Charisma Myth*, author Olivia Fox Cabane dispels the misconception that charisma is something only boisterous and outgoing people have. In fact, one of the most fascinating findings of her book is that people are rated as more charismatic relative to how awesome they make *other people feel* when they are around.

Isn't that amazing news?

Charisma is way less about you and way more about how you make others feel. And you make other people feel great by creating genuine connection and rapport. You make genuine connections when you are your most natural version of yourself. We are going to get deeply connected with your most natural style of expression in a moment.

Charisma is way less about you and way more about how you make others feel.

The first thing to do is recognize the most charisma-depleting culprit of all—our old foe: speaking anxiety.

Speaking anxiety management strategies are discussed in more depth in Chapter 15 so I will refer you there for the full discussion and many tools. For now, simply recognize that no matter how well you understand your own style and feel committed to authentic expression, until you put strategies in place to release speaking anxiety, you won't be able to physically or mentally step into your most naturally charismatic self. Thankfully, fear and anxiety-reducing strategies really do work—so you can do this!

Now, let's explore your own natural style. This exercise is a client favorite by a long shot. It's just so much fun—and so enlightening—when you put exciting words around who you are when you are at your best.

EXERCISE: YOUR EXPRESSION ÉLAN (AKA: YOUR NATURAL EXPRESSION STYLE)

Grab your journal so you can take some notes at the end of this exercise. Close your eyes and think back to the last time you were in a small group conversation you really enjoyed. This can be at work or in your personal life. It should be a time when you were thinking to yourself something like, "This is really fun! I'm loving this conversation."

Remember who was there, and what you all were talking about. Tap into the energy you felt. Recall the feelings you experienced in your body during this conversation.

Now, watch this conversation, with you in it, as if on a movie screen behind your eyes. Notice the way you were *being* in the conversation. What words would you use to describe your way of being (not what you were saying, just *how you were being*).

You might choose words like:

Funny, smart, intellectual, reflective, compassionate, curious...it could be anything, but it must be positive. After all, you are really enjoying this conversation, which means you like the way you are being in it, too. Just jot down three of the words you would use to describe the way you were being in your journal.

Once you have chosen three words, take those words to the thesaurus. You can use a paper thesaurus, or an online thesaurus like **www. thesaurus.com**.

In the thesaurus, look deeper at the synonyms of each word to see if there is an even better word to describe the way you are being in that conversation.

Dig three layers deep to try to find the very best words for the way you are being. For example, if your word is "funny," you might discover "witty" and decide that is an even better word to describe the way you were being in that conversation you loved so much.

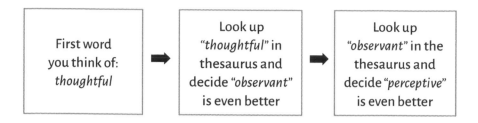

| First word you think of: *thoughtful* | Look up *"thoughtful"* in thesaurus and decide *"observant"* is even better | Look up *"observant"* in the thesaurus and decide *"perceptive"* is even better |

Note that while you are only using one scenario, it is useful because this scenario represents the way you are when you are communicating at your best. When you feel that great in conversation, you are almost always connected with your most natural style of expression.

Combinations of words you come up with might look like:

Word #1	**Word #2**	**Word #3**
Entertaining	*Thoughtful*	*Edgy*
Light	*Flowing*	*Mysterious*
Deep	*Wandering*	*Grounded*

These three words—which I call your Expression Élan words (*élan* is a French word which means enthusiastic style)—can help you connect more powerfully when you communicate, in speaking and in all of your engagements. They do this by guiding you to be even *more yourself*.

The full Expression Élan process is a much deeper dive into your own natural expression style and an even richer application for your speaking and thought leadership. You can access that deeper dive process through the book resources page at **beyondapplausebook.com/resources**.

Here are the most important things to know about your Expression Élan:

1. They are your words and no one else gets to weigh in on them in any way. *You* decide what words describe you at your best.
2. These words must lift you up and make you want to be more of the qualities you associate with them.

What are the three Expression Élan words you landed on after your the-saurus search? Write them in your journal.

But wait, you aren't done yet! It gets even better from here.

Spend a few moments with each word, describing for yourself what you mean by it. Choose some colors, images, and feelings that the words evoke for you. It doesn't matter that your definitions or any of the ele-ments you lay out make any sense to anyone else but you. Make some notes in your journal using the following table as a guide.

	Word #1	Word #2	Word #3
What I mean by this word:			
Colors			
Images			
Feelings			

Now that you have these words that describe the way you are being when you are expressing in your most natural charismatic way, and you have colors, images and feelings that being that way brings to mind for you, you can infuse these qualities into all of your thought leadership going forward.

With your Expression Élan words to support you, you can be even more conscious about who you are being when you are communicating at your best.

The second half of your greatest natural charisma comes from releas-ing any speaking anxiety that's blocking your full expression. Again, just as was discussed about conviction, once you manage that speaking anxiety, you will find yourself connecting more deeply with your audience. (Remember to refer to Chapter 15 for some awesome fear-releasing strategies.)

EXERCISE: YOUR CHARISMA IN ACTION

In the first exercise, you gave yourself some exciting labels to name your own natural charisma style. How do you plan to use those words to express in the most authentic captivating and engaging way? Make a plan for yourself in your journal. Below are some examples of ways to activate your Expression Élan words:

- Infuse words and phrases from your Expression Élan into your talk to add spice and energy to the language.
- Add images and colors to your slides; bring objects or other stage decorations that come from your Expression Élan exercise so the experience of your talk feels richer through these personally inspired elements.
- Choose the outfit for your next speaking event using the colors in your Expression Élan to help you bring some of that energy and feeling to your talk.
- Tell a story in your next talk that evokes the feeling words you revealed in your Expression Élan exercise to help bring that authentic feeling energy to your talk delivery and audience experience.

Chapter Eleven

CRAFTING YOUR TRANSFORMATIONAL
THOUGHT LEADERSHIP TALK

*I*f you visit your favorite book retailer, you will find plenty of books on how to craft and deliver a great talk. In fact, I wrote one of those books myself. The variety of books available is wonderful because you have many choices for the style of book you want to teach you how to structure your talk, choose the best content, and give you tips and strategies on speaking delivery.

While we will touch on some of the essential elements of a great talk, this book is about the level beyond that. It's about your impact, the difference you make through your speaking, and, really, all of your thought leadership. I know that you either already know how to structure a great talk or you are fully confident that you can find that information easily, and I don't want to spend your precious time going over those details.

Instead this chapter will focus on how to brighten your speaking in every way—how to speak like the transformational thought leader that you are meant to be.

The thing is, thought leaders, especially those who are committed to transformation for their audiences, do things differently than those who are focused only on the art and craft of speaking.

> Transformational Thought Leaders do things differently than those who are focused only on the art and craft of speaking.

Transformational thought leaders bring new ideas and new ways of sharing their ideas. They are committed not just to sharing the best content, but to bringing the very best of themselves when they share that content. That's why you are reading this book—because you are committed to that kind of impact through your speaking.

PREPARING TO CRAFT YOUR THOUGHT LEADERSHIP TALK

First things first. When you are ready to create your talk, you must walk away from your computer. You'll have to trust me on this because it may go against what feels like your instinct (but is really just a habit you likely learned from someone else). Your most creative ideas live and breathe far away from your day-to-day workspace and your computer.

The problem with starting at your computer is that most people have a habit of thinking linearly when sitting in front of a computer. One thing follows the other. There is a logical sequence of activities that you do on your computer to get you to your goal. That is the exact opposite kind of thinking that you need in order to craft the most captivating presentation, the kind that lights up your audience and sets you up as a thought leader in your industry.

Okay, action time! Grab these items:

- A pencil
- Notepad
- Sticky notes
- A folder
- Optional: large flip chart paper

98

Choose a location that is totally different than where you normally work at your computer. This may mean going into your backyard, or it could mean walking to a nearby park or a coffee shop. It can also mean a different room in your house or office space. The point is to shake up your surroundings.

Brainstorming to Reveal Your Best Talk Content

In your new surroundings, you're going to ask yourself this question: *What is everything I could say about this topic?*

Here are two ways to get at the answer to that question in the most fruitful way.

Pen and Paper Approach

If you'd like to start with your notebook and paper, just jot down every single idea that comes to mind related to the topic of your talk. At this point, you don't have to know how you will use the ideas you write down. For now, you're just brainstorming, which means you're writing down every single thing that comes to your mind. You can do this in list format or you can do this with a mind map.

Sticky Note Approach

If you're using the large, flip-chart sized paper and sticky notes approach, you'll simply write each idea on a sticky note and place it on the large paper. If you prefer something more easily portable, place the sticky notes inside of the folder you brought with you. Just stick them right inside the covers of that folder. No order or neatness required at this point.

There are unique benefits to each approach. The cool thing about the folder approach is that you can then fold up that folder and carry those notes around with you for the next time you want to work on your talk. With the large paper and sticky notes, you can leave your initial brainstorm where it is and walk away from it for a while. As you walk past that brainstorm over time, new ideas will likely show up and you can easily add them to the brainstorm by adding a new sticky note. Of course, you can do this with the folder, too, it's just usually tucked away somewhere and less likely to prompt spontaneous engagement.

After you've revealed everything you can think of and gotten it written down, take a break. Go for a walk. Celebrate that you have started! And know this: you are already approaching your topic in a more innovative way than the vast majority of speakers—and even thought leaders. This brainstorm content (and the additional content likely to flow as a result of your mind-opening approach) is going to be gold for your talk crafting process. You will come back to this when it's time to craft your outline.

Before you craft your outline, though, you need to get deeply connected with your audience.

Understanding the Audience for a Specific Speaking Event

So far in this book we have talked about how to best serve your Ideal Audience Member through speaking. In the perfect scenario, you can use those same Ideal Audience Exercises to guide the content of your upcoming talks.

However, in practice, you will be crafting talks for audiences that are similar, but not necessarily exactly like, your Ideal Audience Member. Often times, your audience is actually even more specific than you described in your Ideal Audience Member Exercises and, therefore, some fun details will arise as you explore their struggles and life experiences. These can inform your overall understanding of your Ideal Audience Member as well.

For example, let's say your upcoming speaking event is for a national personal trainer's association conference. Since you are a naturopathic doctor, the audience members at the conference are excited to learn new strategies they can share with their clients for living a healthier lifestyle overall. While you often speak to wellness groups, the unique focus on physical fitness of this group inspires you to dive deeper into the thoughts, ideas, struggles, and barriers to health that are unique to personal trainers and their clients. Placing more attention on these specifics helps you tell stories and share medical knowledge about posture and the relationship between muscle mass and energy that you rarely share in your talks with groups who are more focused on nutrition.

Once you know the specific speaking event where you will deliver your talk, take yourself through the Ideal Audience Member Exercises in Chapter 6 to get as connected as possible to the thoughts, feelings, and experiences of the audience who will be at this specific event. Having this information at the ready as you craft a custom version of Your Rooftop Message Talk for this audience will ensure that you delight them with the details in your talk.

CRAFTING YOUR ROOFTOP MESSAGE TALK

You are armed with a rich connection with the audience for whom you are crafting your talk—and a plethora of ideas for content. Now, it's time to create your awesome customized Rooftop Message Talk to delight this particular audience.

Your Talk Outline

Most speakers create their talks in one of two ways. They either start by sitting down with a presentation slide software program, such as PowerPoint® or Keynote®, and map out the content that way. Or, they write out their talk fully freeform. Every once in a while I meet someone who starts by mapping out an outline. If this is you, then HIGH-FIVE! This is the best way to begin crafting a captivating talk.

A quick search online will reveal many types of outlines you can use. It matters less which type of outline, as long as it makes sense for the content and your speaking goals. I share an outline structure with clients and organizations that I call "The Only Presentation Outline You'll Ever Need" (TOPOYEN). That simple outline is gold. I have clients tell me years after our work together that they still pull out that outline every single time they map out a new talk. (If you'd like a copy of that outline with instructions on how to fill it out, go to our book resources page at **beyondapplausebook. com/resources** to download your copy.)

The reason I strongly recommend using an outline is that it allows you to see the whole picture of your talk in one place.

An outline allows you to see the whole picture of your talk in one place.

It's easy to see the mix of your content and where you may need more captivation techniques (more on those soon) to keep your audience engaged.

The essentials of your outline are:

- Introduction
- Thesis statement (built from your Thought Leadership Stand)
- Main points (usually three; see my TOPOYEN outline on the online book resources page at **beyondapplausebook.com/resources** for an example)
- Support points (this is where the magic comes in; see below in "Magic Mix of Content")
- Conclusion (Summary, call to action, leave the audience totally inspired and excited to do something new and great!)

Introduction

Your audience decides in under a minute whether they like and trust you enough to pay attention to you.

Your audience decides in under a minute whether they like and trust you enough to pay attention to you.

It's not personal, it's a survival instinct. The brain is on a continuous mission to keep you alive, tirelessly searching for cues on this mission, which means it needs to make quick decisions about where to place attention and where it can conserve energy. Your audience members' brains are simply asking this question at the start of your talk.

This means you need to pay special attention to everything you do in the first few minutes of your presentation. Your main job is to inspire connection, trust, and confidence that the experience and information the audience is about to receive will serve them in a way that matters.

Here are three ways to evoke trust and connection with your audience members in your introduction:

1. Tell a story that immediately shows you understand them and the struggles they are experiencing, and which establishes your credibility in helping them solve their problem (more on this below).
2. Facilitate a short discussion with the audience—a show of hands, or quick question with audience response—that orients the conversation to show that you will be solving a problem that matters to them.
3. Invite audience members into an activity that immediately taps into the problem they are experiencing in a way that delights them and inspires confidence in your ability to help them solve it.

While there are many ways to craft a compelling introduction to your talk, there is special power in using your own experience and story, if they are relevant. Since it is common for my clients to be sharing their own experiences in their thought leadership talks, I created the "I Get It" Intro to guide them in crafting their talk introductions.

You may find this format useful in your own thought leadership talk.

Your "I Get It" Intro

Have you ever been sitting in the audience listening to a speaker when suddenly your jaw drops or you burst out in laughter because what they are describing is so familiar, so much like your own experience that you are astounded? That's the power of an "I Get It" Intro.

The purpose of the "I Get It" Intro is to let your audience know that you understand what they may be experiencing, and that you are qualified and ready to help.

The "I Get It" Intro is to let your audience know that you understand what they may be experiencing, and that you are qualified and ready to help.

Approaching your introduction in this way encourages trust and connection, both of which are very important for inspiring action.

The format of your "I Get It" Intro looks like this:

1. Their current reality: "I get it..." (describe what they are experiencing)
2. What they so want: "Yet you want..." (describe in detail what they want, and, if relevant, recognize that it's really not that much to ask to want this...)

3. Why it's hard for them: "You are not alone... this is why this is just a really hard problem for so many of us..."

4. How/Why You get it: "I know because I've been there..." (if this is true, share a quick and very relevant version of your story. Remember, it's about making a connection with your Ideal Audience Member. Don't get too caught up in details that don't help create connection with them.) OR "I know because I have helped many... " (and share some short example stories of others you've worked with who struggled similarly)

5. There is hope: "I'm on the other side..." OR "I've helped many people solve this... you can do this, too."

6. Here's how to get what they want: "Let me help you, starting now..." (Share your main points from your outline that begin the solution for them.)

When sharing your "I Get It" Intro it's important to balance the exciting outcomes you experienced with the reality of what it took to get there. Even more than the "results not typical" fine print you see on weight loss ads, you want to be clear about the work it took to reach your goals. You don't want to weigh down the whole introduction with heavy detail—you're just getting started after all!—but you do want to present the full picture so the audience can assess where they stand in their willingness and desire to take successful action.

Whether you use the "I Get It" Intro or not, the key elements of your introduction are: making a connection with the audience; orienting them to the topic you are covering; and establishing your credibility as someone who can serve them meaningfully in solving their problem.

If you have done these three things in your introduction well, you will inspire trust and a hopefulness and anticipation for the rest of your talk in your audience.

Thesis Statement

The thesis statement is the one central idea of your talk, and it is derived directly from your Thought Leadership Stand (revisit Chapter 4 to reacquaint with this concept).

I'd like to emphasize something essential here: *one main idea*. I know this sounds very simple—and a bit like we are hailing back to high school English class—but honestly, it's one of the problems with many talks I see as I sit in the audience. It happens at every level and in just about every topic area. Speakers are trying to cover too many things, and, as a result, the audience gets lost in the content and the speaker loses their attention. It's hard to come back from that, for the speaker or the audience.

Your talk must be crafted around one single thesis statement, which drives all of the content in the rest of your talk.

The way to decide on your thesis statement is to go back to your Thought Leadership Stand from Chapter 4. Be sure you are connected with the stand you are taking and with your message to the world.

Then, use the exercises you completed from "Understanding the Audience for a Specific Speaking Event" in this chapter to reveal the specific needs and wants of that particular audience. Pay special attention to the words this audience uses to describe their struggle and, where possible, infuse your thesis with those words. Hearing their own words come from your mouth is a powerful connector.

The combination of these two elements creates your thesis.

Here are examples of thesis statements for talks with specific audiences:

- Increasing muscle mass shapes the body *and* the mind. (Speaker: Naturopathic doctor, Audience: personal trainers)
- Do one thing every day to have the most productive year of your life. (Speaker: Productivity expert, Audience: Business leaders)
- Five minutes to a more loving and passionate marriage. (Speaker: Therapist, Audience: Couples at a relationship retreat)

- You are creative, you just forgot how. (Speaker: neuroscientist, Audience: personal development conference)

Main Points

The main points of your talk all serve to expand upon or support your thesis statement. If you go back and do the brainstorming exercise from earlier in this chapter, you will see that you have a rich treasure chest of material you can use in this talk.

Spend a few minutes putting those brainstormed ideas into categories or themes (the sticky note approach makes this much easier). See what naturally comes to mind when you group those ideas together. This is often an effective way to decide on the main points of your talk. When the content itself shows you the best support for your talk, you are in a golden situation.

It doesn't always work this way, though. Sometimes you already know exactly what your main support points will be for your talk. When this is the case, use the brainstorm content to flesh out the support points, which are discussed below.

This is another time where your clarity and brevity are essential. The brain can only handle so much information. As a rule, stick to no more than three main points.

Yes, only three main points, and almost all the time.

If you are like many of my clients and students, you may be thinking that in your particular circumstance it makes sense to have five main points. But very rarely is it better to have more than three main points because our brains can't remember much more than that. There is significant research to support the value of minimizing the amount of content. John Medina's book, *Brain Rules: 12 Principles for Surviving and Thriving at Work, Home and School* is a great place to get an introduction to this principle. If you do decide to go with more than three main points, you must come up with some way to help your audience remember the points you are covering. You could use an acronym or some other memory tool, but you've got to give them something to help them remember.

For the vast majority of topics, though, three main points is the magic number—and this is the number you will find in my TOPOYEN outline template which you can now access on the book resources page at **beyondapplausebook.com/resources**. (Clients love this outline template—be sure to download yours!)

For the vast majority of topics three main points is the magic number.

In case you find it helpful to see this structure for a talk in action, great examples are available online. Steve Jobs' Stanford commencement speech uses three stories in the body of his speech. In Sheryl Sandberg's TED talk, *Why We Have Too Few Women Leaders*, she lays out a very clear three-part structure. *The 3 A's of Awesome* TED Talk by Neil Pasricha is also a great example of using this rule of three in speech structure.

Support Points

Once you have the main structure of your talk in place, you need to fill it with supporting content: *captivating, engaging and useful content*. Thank goodness you did that brainstorm process and have all of those juicy nuggets to pull from for your talk outline.

What I'm about to say may be the most important shift you make in the way you approach crafting your talks: *It's not about what you know.*

It's common to approach content with the question "What do I know? What could I say to help explain what I have promised to talk about today?" Answering that question will probably lead to a good talk, but likely not very exciting talk. The real question to ask yourself as you think about the content to fill in your talk is: *What does this audience desperately want to know? How can I share this information in a way that lights up, delights, and powerfully moves this audience?*

When you ask these questions in this way, you invite your heart, soul, and brain to conspire together to bring you the very best content for this particular audience. This ensures that they are at the center of your planning, not you and what you know. This is such a critical distinction. If you get just this one thing right, your talk will already be way ahead of the vast majority of talks your audience has experienced.

Notice that in asking these questions I didn't say, "What does this audience desperately *need* to know?" You've got to give them what they want before you can give them what they need.

You've got to give them what they want before you can give them what they need.

This is a fundamental truth in business—and human connection overall. You make the connection with your audience by recognizing and honoring what they are most wanting, and then, when you have built genuine connection and trust, you are more likely to be given permission to offer to them what they really need.

Here's an example of how this plays out in a real talk. Let's say you are an executive coach for entrepreneurs in high-tech and you are speaking at an innovation conference. Your audience is mostly leaders and founders in emerging high-tech companies. Your Thought Leadership Stand is that the greatest innovation only arises during time and space away from the office. Your audience at this conference is currently working ten-hour days, six or seven days a week. How open do you think they will be to you leading with the message, "You must get away from the office for multiple days in a row if you want to create the most innovative products"? Chances are, they will choose the "Get more done in less time" breakout session, or sit in the lobby and respond to some of the thousands of emails in their inbox instead.

You know that what they *need* is to get away from the office. However, what they *want* is to create mind-blowingly awesome products while staying on top of the many other aspects of running a growing company. You must lead with what they want in order to earn the right to offer them what you know they really need. With this in mind, your talk title could be: *Fast and Furious Innovation: How to Generate Product Ideas that Blow the Minds of Your Customers in Record Time.*

Important note here: you must deliver on the promise of your talk. I'm not talking about a bait and switch here. I'm talking about crafting your talk to lead them from what they are currently wanting to seeing and believing in what you know will genuinely help them get to the goal that is at the heart of what they want. You can do this with integrity and credibility because you are an expert. You've done it yourself or with your clients and, therefore, have insight and knowledge that your audience doesn't have yet. This is the great gift of sharing your content mastery as a thought leader.

ENHANCING YOUR TALK WITH THE MAGIC MIX OF CONTENT

I call the process of enhancing your outline with content "blossoming your outline." I think of blossoming like the magic that we weave into an audience's experience. That's why it's called "The Magic Mix of Content." The goal in blossoming is to light up all areas of the brain, as well as the audience members' hearts.

While there are so many ways you can blossom a talk outline, the main overarching categories are:

1. Stories
2. Research & Data

3. Audience engagement activities
4. Compelling visuals

Using a mix of these types of support will give you the very best chance of captivating and inspiring your audience to action.

Using the magic mix of content will give you the very best chance of captivating and inspiring your audience to action.

Stories. Well-told stories are a powerful way to captivate hearts and minds in your speaking. In fact, fascinating research has shown how stories sync up our brains in very unique ways, allowing us to understand each other more deeply. Experientially, well chosen stories show that you understand their experience, creating stronger connection.

We also know that lessons taught through story are far more likely to be remembered, making storytelling a powerful teaching tool. When we use a story intentionally and with the right details, the learning comes through with more ease and grace as well.

Finally (although there is so much more we could say about story), well-told stories that include a complete story arc motivate people to action, especially in combination with data or research evidence. The emotional component so often a part of a well-told story pulls on the heart as well as the mind—a powerful combination to inspire action.

While research certainly backs up these claims about the power of storytelling, that research is simply reinforcing what we already know is true from generations upon generations of folklore storytelling. Throughout this book I share stories in service of inspiring the same kind of engagement and memory enhancement described here.

Research & Data. Think of how fascinating it is when you hear a shocking research finding. This happened to me recently when Mama CEO founder, Megan Flatt, started reading off statistics about how mothers are perceived at work by leaders and colleagues. No wonder mothers struggle to get promoted! (Do a search, I bet you'll be shocked, too.) There is nothing like credible research to highlight and reinforce something that we suspected was true—or to help you get on board when you are being told something that shocks you. "Really?!," we say to ourselves. "YES!" says the research.

Research is also valuable for balancing out the very personal nature of storytelling. When you hear a story that moves you, and then it's supported with research that confirms that is not just that one person in that one story, you are much more likely to take action on the new information you are learning.

The most effective approach is to use research in combination with your stories for maximum effect. This is part of the magic in what I call the "Magic Mix of Content."

Audience Engagement Activities. At a big conference a couple years ago, the speaker opened by asking each of us to share a dream for our life with someone near us who we didn't know. It was daunting at first, but I have to admit, it made me feel more connected to the people in the room that day. Inviting your audience to do something with the material you are covering helps them get invested in the learning.

Audience engagement activities also help you remember the content that you're sharing because any time you interact directly with the content, the content gets more imprinted for memory. Since the goal is to help the audience not only stay engaged, but also to be able to take positive action in their lives after they leave the room, this is valuable. This is why I always have my workshop attendees stand up and practice body movement with me when we talk about speaking delivery skills. When it's time for them to deliver their talks, they are more likely to remember the strategies I taught them because they have both a mental and a physical memory of the learning.

Here's the truth: It is hard to sit and listen to someone speak for an extended period of time, no matter what the topic. Even when the speaker is captivating and full of valuable information, sitting and passively taking in information is hard to do for very long. That is why audience engagement activities are so powerful for great speaking.

Compelling Visuals. Much like stories, compelling relevant images captivate the brain and the heart. In fact, brain scientists tell us that at least half of our brains are dedicated to visual processing. When you see an image, a whole lot of the brain is engaged. When that image is attached to great content, you get the benefit of the Picture Superiority Effect (PSA), a concept John Medina talks about in his excellent book *Brain Rules*, which I referred to earlier. The PSA says we have a 65% likelihood of remembering content delivered with an image and text or audio combo, compared to 10% likelihood with audio or text and no images. See, the brain just loves images.

Conclusion

While your captivating introduction gets the audience's attention, your persuasive and powerful conclusion will dramatically impact their motivation to act as a result of your talk.

While your captivating introduction gets the audience's attention, your persuasive and powerful conclusion will dramatically impact their motivation to act as a result of your talk.

Since your goal is to make a difference in the lives of those you are meant to serve, your conclusion is a critical part of your talk.

The secret to a great conclusion to your talk is to quickly yet effectively remind the audience of the most important takeaways. This may mean a review of your three main points, or a reiteration of the importance of your main idea. This doesn't mean going back into the details, of course—be careful of this. Too many conclusions go on too long. Once your audience can feel the start of your conclusion, they are orienting toward the completion of your talk. You want to conclude before they are finished listening so make it catchy, clear, and quick!

These are valuable elements in your conclusion, depending on the goals of your talk:

- **A clear call to action.** If you want your audience to sign-up to your email list to download a free resource, or to donate to your non-profit organization, for example, send them to a simple website address where they can sign-up immediately after your talk concludes.
- **Share a quick inspiring story that lifts their spirits and activates them in a specific way.** Share a success story about someone who struggled with exactly what they are struggling with, and make the connection to their own opportunity for success very clear in that story. A fun variation on this is to introduce the story early in your talk but don't tell the outcome—leave them hanging, in a playful and intriguing way. As you conclude your talk, refer back to that early story, saying, "Remember the story about... Well let me tell you what happened for him..." The brain loves a puzzle and loves to be delighted. When the two come together, it's a double win for attention and motivation!
- **Always close with gratitude for your audience.** A simple "thank you" is lovely and honors their time, attention, and the connection you've built.

While your outline may have one or two elements not listed in this section, the vast majority of the time these are all you need. And with speaking, as with so many things, simplicity is where the magic happens.

There is a remaining important element of a powerful thought leadership talk that I haven't covered yet—mostly because its placement varies depending on the audience and your goals. This element is your own Story of Transformation.

Sometimes you will use your Story of Transformation in your "I Get It" Intro, and other times you will stay more general with your story in your intro and choose to share the full story later. There will be times when your own Story of Transformation isn't nearly as useful as using a client story as a cornerstone of your talk, in which case you may only refer to your own story in very general terms. Regardless, knowing how to tell your Story of Transformation is essential to your role as a Transformational Thought Leader.

YOUR STORY OF TRANSFORMATION

There is a good chance that you are doing this work because you experienced a significant transformation in your own life in the area of your expertise. If this is the case, your Story of Transformation is a great gift to your audience. Knowing how to share your story of transformation so that it best serves the audience helps make a powerful impact without turning the attention too much on you.

Brené Brown's Story of Transformation in her wildly popular TED Talk *The Power of Vulnerability* is a big part of what made her talk so compelling. It's so easy to relate to her story about her resistance to being more vulnerable because so many of us feel the same things she felt. As she expresses these feelings through her own details, effectively demonstrating her point about being more vulnerable by doing it herself, you are able to see yourself in her without feeling confronted. It's a gentle yet powerful way to help each of us recognize our own experiences through her story.

You will hear stories of transformation shared by so many speakers, when you start to listen for them. Simon Sinek's story about waking up one morning and realizing he had built a whole business without really knowing if or why it mattered to him is another great example, and the basis of his "Start with Why" thought leadership work. Similarly, Brendan Burchard tells the story of his car accident and how that launched his career in personal development.

In the personal development world, you hear stories of transformation all the time. I've heard many business-building gurus encourage people to tell stories in a highly dramatic way, even so that they are exaggerated. It's easy to think from these often very dramatic stories that you have to have been curled up on the floor in mental and physical breakdown in order to have a story worth telling. But this is not true. For many of us, our own transformation happened over time, with many moments building up to the one in which we said, "Enough! I'm not living like this anymore." Many of us were standing or driving or taking a shower when this happened, not curled up on the floor.

You want to tell the truth of your story, period. And—this is important—even your story in this context is about your audience. (Virtually everything you do in transformational thought leadership speaking is about your audience.) It's crafted and shared for the benefit of the audience feeling less alone, and instead inspired and hopeful. With this goal in heart and mind, you can focus on the details of your story that will resonate for your Ideal Audience Member. It's not about manipulating what happened in your story or leaving out details that significantly affect the outcomes, it's simply about recognizing what parts of your story will serve best and sharing your story in that way.

Even your story in the context of Transformational Thought Leadership is ultimately about the audience.

As a general guideline, your Story of Transformation has four parts:

1. What it was like for you in the midst of the struggle.
2. What happened that inspired/forced/caused a significant shift (often a moment in time).
3. Some detail about how you began to turn things around (it didn't happen overnight).
4. What life is like now on the other side of that transformation (an honest account, of course).

Told well, this story can be a beacon of hope and understanding for your Ideal Audience Member. In the midst of struggle or great desire (which actually also feels like struggle), hearing an honest and inspiring account of coming out the other side whole and better than before just may be the most valuable offering you can share.

Once your talk outline is crafted with all of the appropriate elements to serve your ideal audience, the fun really begins. Now it's time to take your excellent essential content and kick it all up a notch—or three.

ENRICH YOUR TALK WITH CAPTIVATION TECHNIQUES

The brain doesn't pay attention to boring things. It simply checks out. We know this from experience—and our experience is backed up by research. Your charge as a thought leader is to be "not boring" so that the audiences' brains can stay focused on your talk. The question is: how do you do this?

The answer: Take them on an emotional journey, an adventure even. Actively weave an experience into your talk in which the audience will feel a range of emotions such as delight, anticipation, intrigue, hope and inspiration—and also sadness, frustration, and even anger, where appropriate. This is part of why Dr. Martin Luther King Jr.'s "I Have a Dream" speech is so powerful—this is also why modern TED talks often create such impact on the audience. These talks are designed to captivate and inspire.

This is what you want to do, too—captivate and inspire your audience to action. Here's a sampling of some captivation techniques you can weave into your talk:

Share something completely novel. If you want to see a new and totally unexpected amplifying aid, watch Jill Bolte Taylor's TED Talk called "Stroke of Insight." Pay special attention at minute 2:25 to see what I mean.

We love the unexpected. The scientific research that totally surprises your audience fits that bill, like those statistics I heard during Megan Flatt's talk about how mothers are perceived at work. You can also bring in the unexpected through an audience activity, through a story, or through a powerful statistic. Even your own stories of vulnerability, fear, and failure are an effective way to bring the unexpected to your talks.

Social connection. Have audience members meet each other. At a recent conference, in one of the breakout sessions, the speakers had us do an exercise in which we got into groups of three people to practice active listening and observation. After the guided conversation, the speakers had each of us take out our smartphones and search online for "the perfect gift" for our new friends. We wrote the gift ideas on a slip of paper and turned them in to the speakers. As the speakers read aloud the gifts, people were asked to raise their hands when they heard a gift that they thought was likely chosen for them. We were all really into this exercise. It was a such a clever and unexpected way to teach us how active listening can result in having others feel really known and understood. Just as valuable, we each had two new friends at the conference, which increased the sense of belonging and connection—what most of us are deeply seeking in our lives.

Use strategic pauses. One of my favorite moments when I deliver a talk is at the very beginning when I share a "Hello Smile" with the audience. This is a three-beat pause after I walk to the front of the group and I look at my audience and make a real connection. I see their faces and we share a smile. I find it starts the talk on a much warmer footing than when I used to just leap into speaking.

Pauses can be used in a variety of ways. When you say something particularly important that you want the audience to remember, pause afterward. They will automatically review what you just said in their own minds and replay it. A pause is an indicator that something good or important is about to happen, or just happened. This is why it's also a good idea to pause before you say something especially powerful. The audiences' brains get active, waiting in suspense for the big reveal.

Even unplanned pauses handled well can be awesome. If you lose your train of thought or you need to find a slide or a note in your stack of papers, pausing with confidence will show that you've got this. As long as it doesn't go on too long, it's a great sign of competence for your audience. The key is to not fill this pause with a stream of words or apologies. If the pause is going on a bit long, give them something to do or think about. As a steward of the audience's experience, your main job is to take care to give them the richest, most useful experience possible. Pauses can add to that experience immensely.

Repeat yourself on purpose. The I Have a Dream speech by Martin Luther King, Jr. is a classic example of repetition used powerfully. Oprah repeats herself on purpose a lot, too, when she has a particularly delightful insight during an interview.

If you want to be sure your audience takes away a particular phrase or mantra from your talk, repeat it. Say it at the end of each paragraph or section. Start with it and end with it. Say it once and then again for emphasis. Our brains love to know what matters. Repetition tells our brain, "Note this! It matters enough to say it again!"

Take them into a scene or feeling with rich description. When you take your audience members on a visual journey in their mind, you increase the impact of your content. In an article for the New York Times called *Your Brain on Fiction*, author Annie Murphy Paul shares abundant research supporting the idea that rich description lights up many areas of our brain, deepening our engagement and connection with the content. This is a very good reason to use rich description when you really want your audience to deeply understand a concept and then remember it.

Gestures and movements that match your words. When you are sitting in the audience mostly passively, seeing the speaker move helps keep your brain engaged. When those movements also assist the audience in understanding what we're saying, they act like an amplifying aid. So if you are talking about the passing of time and you walk in a line, section by section across the front of the stage, the audience can feel you moving through time as you speak. Similarly, if you want the audience to see the size of the flower you grew in your garden, and feel it's fullness more completely without an image, then draw that flower in the air with your hands.

There are many ways to captivate your audience. Use these strategies as a starting place to start weaving in as many captivation techniques as you can that make sense with your audience and content.

Your audience shows up because they believe you will deliver on the promise you put forth in your talk title and description. They want to solve a problem, learn something new, be inspired in a way that matters to them. Once they are there, though, they need so much more in order to truly get the most out of their time with you. They need your best content, woven specially and strategically to delight them. That's what you will give them when you weave in these captivation techniques.

EXERCISE: CRAFT YOUR THOUGHT LEADERSHIP TALK OUTLINE

This chapter is all about crafting your talk with a heart full of service. The best action you can take is to start pulling that talk together. Follow this summary to guide you in this talk crafting exercise:

1. Go somewhere lovely and inspiring and do a content brainstorm.
2. Visit my book resources page **beyondapplausebook.com/resources** and download the outline format to begin crafting your outline.
3. Fill in the main points, intro, and conclusion on that outline.
4. Blossom that outline with awesome content.
5. Start practicing like crazy, infusing captivating techniques along the way.
6. Celebrate! You are on your way to making the biggest impact possible with your message.

The first two steps in this second half of the book are focused on the content of the stand you take and crafting a captivating, engaging, and transformational talk. These are essential steps for any thought leader. But unless and until you get out there in the world and share that stand and offer up your talk, all you have is a highly persuasive conversation with yourself.

To make a meaningful difference with your message, you've got to go where they gather and serve. This is your final step on The Path to Thought Leadership—and it's one you never stop taking.

GO WHERE
THEY GATHER

and

SERVE

Chapter Twelve

SPEAKING TO SERVE

*R*obin Kramer is a business coach for jewelry business owners. She and her business partner, Tracy, run Flourish & Thrive Academy. Robin took the time this year to craft a thought leadership talk in service of jewelry business owners who want to enjoy greater ease and success in their businesses. In the first rendition of her talk at a recent glass bead conference, Robin attracted many of the attendees in the room to join her community at Flourish & Thrive. What's most exciting about this is that now that these new members are in her community, Robin can continue to serve them beyond the walls of that speaking room.

This is the opportunity that comes with going where your Ideal Audience Members gather and serving them in all the ways you can.

For Robin, serving means not only helping them with the tools and strategies she shares in her thought leadership talk, but for those who want a deeper experience, it means inviting them to become clients in her business. This may or may not be the case for you and your thought leadership goals.

My client, Fawzi, who lives in Kuwait, is committed to serving as a speaker and as a mentor for young leaders and entrepreneurs. When he speaks at an event, he shares his best stories and life lessons from across his many years in rising leadership through to his current experience as

CEO of his organization. His goal is to help positively influence the future of the leaders in his country and speaking is a powerful way to help him reach this goal.

In this chapter I'll share with you how to find the best speaking opportunities, as well as how to use each event to lead you to the next great speaking opportunity. I'll also discuss what it means to "serve" at these events, as a speaker and beyond. Finally, I am going to discuss the many kinds of gatherings where you can serve, both online and offline.

WHERE TO FIND THE BEST SPEAKING OPPORTUNITIES

I'll never forget my first conference experience. On my way out of one of my "dark night of the soul" phases in my late twenties, I was trying out all kinds of holistic health practices to help me heal: massage, energy healing, flower essences, thought work, spiritual exploration—you name it, I was into it. It felt like I was discovering a whole underground world that was swirling among us on this Earth but that most of us couldn't see.

It was in the midst of this exploratory period that I attended my first spirituality and wellness conference and my mind was blown. Around every corner and in every speaking room I discovered a new healing or life-affirming modality, a new way of learning about and exploring the human experience. I loved it.

In the decades since that first experience, the types of conference I attend has grown. I'm still a believer in energy work and holistic health, and I also frequent leadership, personal development, and conscious business conferences. In the rooms of these conferences, I get inspired and served powerfully by some of my most important mentors and teachers. I am among hundreds and sometimes thousands of people who are there for the same reasons. (I suspect we've probably been together at some of these conferences, you and me.)

When we have a compelling desire or an intense need, most of us seek out solutions. Many of these solutions are found in gatherings with others.

The goal here is for you to seek out places where your Ideal Audience Members are already gathering so that you can meet them, learn more about them, and, where appropriate, offer to serve in various ways.

Now, I know this sounds a lot like networking—and essentially it is, but when done with heart and a genuine desire to connect, it's a wonderful way to find opportunities to serve with your thought leadership. Here are some of the kinds of gatherings you may want to attend:

Conferences and Association Meetings. These are common places to start. There are conferences around every single topic area that you can imagine. In fact, if you search topics important to your Ideal Audience Member plus the word "association" there is a very good chance that you will find multiple organizations.

Workshops. Workshops are a wonderful place to meet other people in a very interactive environment. Since workshops are usually focused on "how to" there is often time spent working with others. This can make it easier to make meaningful connections with people at the event.

I'd like to make a special note here about going to events hosted by others. If you are at a workshop put on by someone who is in your same area of expertise working with the same audience, you want to be careful about the way you invite further connection with people at the event. I know you wouldn't do it on purpose, but it's worth recognizing the respectful approach we must take here. You definitely don't want to become known as someone who steals potential clients from event hosts.

Local gyms. Especially if your expertise is in fitness, nutrition, or wellness, your local gym can be a fantastic place to make connections that could lead to speaking opportunities.

Churches. Churches are a wonderful place to offer personal development topics, spiritual topics, and even topics of wellness and family. If you are associated with a church, this can be a great opportunity to offer a talk or maybe cover one of the Sunday sermons when the minister is out of town. Of course, your talk will be designed appropriate to the circumstances and likely without an overt business objective, but it's a great way to practice speaking and start becoming known as a speaker in your topic area.

Mom's groups. My awesome professional organizer and friend, Brenna, who owns One Organized Girl™, often speaks to local MOPS (Mothers of Preschoolers, a surprisingly large network of mom meetings across the world) groups and other family focused gatherings because she loves to help busy families organize their lives so they can enjoy their time together more. This is a great source of new clients for Brenna as well as a way that she gets new speaking gigs. If your Ideal Audience Member is a mom, Mom's groups may be an excellent place for you to offer to speak.

Additional locations. There are so many more places and ways that people gather. Here are a few more to get your creative juices flowing. You may even want to hop over to your journal now while you are thinking about it and start jotting down a list of places that you may want to speak. Here are more ideas to add to your brainstorm:

- Yoga or spiritual centers
- Hobby classes
- Social clubs (singles groups, couples' groups, wine clubs)
- Parties and gatherings
- Meetups focused on hobbies
- Chambers of Commerce
- Business networking events
- Local community gatherings

It's a great start to brainstorm all the places people gather. The question is, how do you know where your Ideal Audience Members gather?

Return to your intimate connection with your Ideal Audience Member and what they need and want. Get re-acquainted with your Ideal Audience Member by answering some questions about their struggles and desires, as well as their life overall.

EXERCISE: YOUR IDEAL AUDIENCE MEMBERS AND WHERE THEY GATHER

First, return to your journal entry about Your Ideal Audience Member from Chapter 6 (maybe you even have an Ideal Audience Member drawing—that's ideal!)

Imagine this person were sitting with you at a coffee shop, telling you about what's difficult in their life. What is this person saying to you in this conversation?

Of course, at least some of the things they are struggling with relate to your message, otherwise they wouldn't be your Ideal Audience Member. But don't limit yourself to just the problems you solve. Lay it all out there about their struggles in a brainstorm list, starting with what you have in your journal from your Ideal Audience Member exercises in Chapter 6. Write it all out so it's all in one place for you to do this exercise on where they gather.

If you took yourself through the Ideal Audience Member exercises in Chapter 6, you will have a bounty of thoughts to note here. It's important to be deeply connected with what they are struggling with at this stage because you need to answer the question, "Where does this person *go* to try to solve this problem?" This is the essential question at the heart of this exercise.

Use the prompts below to write down as many places as you can think of, and feel free to guess like crazy. It's all just a brainstorm at this point. Don't worry if these gathering places aren't specifically related to your topic.

Use your journal to record your ideas for the following prompts:

Where does he or she go for...

...work related learning, connection, growth?

...fun in evenings, weekends (or during the day if their hours are non-traditional)?

...personal happiness, joy, pleasure? (hobby shops or hobby workshops, conferences, book stores...)

...health and wellness?

Now let's explore possible solutions to the problems they shared with you in this visualized coffee date. In their intense desire to solve this problem, where might they gather with others to find a solution?

Create the box below in your journal to help you expand your brainstorm of places they might go to try to solve the problem they are experiencing and fill in the quadrants there.

Locally (gym, church, meetups, school, etc.)	**Nationally** (conferences, training, competitions, etc.)
Online (Facebook & LinkedIn groups, discussion boards, other social media, etc.)	**Other** (hobby groups, international gatherings, etc.)

EXERCISE: MAKE YOUR *GO WHERE THEY GATHER* PLAN

Looking over this quadrant exercise, which of these gatherings would you genuinely enjoy attending? Those are your sweet spot places for gathering with your Ideal Audience Members to serve. Write down your favorites in your journal.

Gathering one:

Gathering two:

Gathering three:

When is the next meeting for one or two of these groups? Mark down dates and locations.

Gathering One—event name, date, time and location:

Gathering Two—event name, date, time and location:

What topic customization of your Rooftop Message Talk could you offer to share for these groups? Jot down some talk titles that would light up and delight this group, especially the meeting organizers.

Talk title and description one: _____

_____

_____

Talk title and description two: _____

_____

_____

Talk title and description three: _____

_____

_____

A broad exploration and inquiry into where your Ideal Audience Members gather not only to try to solve the issue you help solve, but also to enjoy their life, opens up many ideas for ways you can serve through speaking. Keep your mind and heart open as you continue to explore opportunities. You will most certainly find yourself enjoying and serving with your speaking in places and on themes you right now can't even imagine. It's one of the most fun parts of expanding your thought leadership. I can't wait to hear your stories of new speaking adventures!

OFFERING TO SERVE

You will likely find that when you let others know at these events that you are a speaker—if you are in fact at a gathering of your Ideal Audience Members—you will be offered totally unexpected speaking opportunities. This happens to my clients all the time.

The important thing is, you must call yourself a speaker in order for the thought to trigger in the other person's mind that they may have you come speak. The other important thing is that you give them time to get to know you before you expect to be invited onto their stages.

Be Ready to Serve

It's a lot of work to figure out where to speak, pull together materials like your speaker page (more on that soon), and compose an email that's enticing enough for a meeting organizer to open much less respond "Yes!"

Yet this work is nothing in the face of your commitment to serve. (If that doesn't feel true, go back to Chapter 7 on Commitment to help you get to that place.) This is what you do to serve at the highest level through speaking. It's an essential part of your calling.

I once attended a fundraising event at the Boys and Girls Club where a neurosurgeon was the opening keynote speaker. He was talking about how hard it is to make systemic change using the analogy of his own medical school education. He said, "You don't become a neurosurgeon by spending a lot of time thinking about what it takes to become one. You become a neurosurgeon by committing to become a neurosurgeon and then meeting with a college counselor and taking the very next step toward becoming a neurosurgeon. Pretty soon when you take step after step after step you find yourself a neurosurgeon."

While thought leadership certainly isn't neuroscience (unless you're a neuroscientist!), his talk describes well the process of becoming a recognized and sought-after thought leader. This is just the way it is with anything big and meaningful that you want to do with your life and work. You don't get there by overwhelming yourself with thinking about everything it will take to get to that end result. You get there by making a powerful commitment and then taking step after step after step toward getting there with everything you've got.

Offer to Speak Often and Generously

Becoming a well-known thought leader takes time, energy, and prolific contribution of your thought leadership through speaking and writing. The fact is, you've got to start somewhere. There is no better place to start than right where you are right now.

As you look over the brainstorm of places your Ideal Audience Members gather that you completed earlier in this chapter, highlight any groups to which you have a current connection. The stronger your connection, the better. These are excellent places for you to begin your speaking and thought leadership journey. Even if you are already speaking regularly, consider these groups as a great place to test out new ideas or serve more deeply with ideas you have shared previously.

Every one of the 5 C's of Thought Leadership Speaking gets strengthened with each opportunity to speak. In fact, without regular and varied speaking experiences, your ideas simply can't flourish as fully. You will learn so much through audience questions and non-verbal responses, feedback from event organizers and your own realizations as you share your ideas in newly refined ways each time.

Speak for free as well as for pay. You will hear arguments against speaking for free from other speaking experts. I have found that, when chosen appropriately, speaking to groups of my Ideal Audience Members, even without a speaking fee, has been financially and emotionally rewarding time and time again. This is true for my clients who use speaking to attract clients as well.

Nothing will help you become a more captivating, inspiring, life-changing speaker than speaking often.

Nothing will help you become a more captivating, inspiring, life-changing speaker than speaking often.

In his book *Outliers: The Story of Success*, Malcolm Gladwell says that it takes 10,000 hours to reach mastery in a particular skill. While a daunting goal, the good news is that you can be a catalyst for meaningful change for many people all along the way of that path to mastery. It just requires that you keep working to become better as a leader and speaker, making your message and delivery increasingly effective in serving your audience members.

You simply can't learn as much about what works and doesn't in your content, what engages the audience and which stories light them up without actually standing before audiences and delivering. This learning is what helps you go from an aspiring thought leader to a sought-after one. As long as you learn and refine after every talk, this is your path to mastery and making the difference you want to make as a thought leader.

What if "No" Simply Means "Not yet"?

Landing speaking opportunities isn't easy. I hear this often and I know it from my own experience as well. Meeting organizers are very careful about who they let on their stages because their reputation is on the line. Their audience is trusting them to provide an engaging, useful and, ideally, delightful experience. If an event organizer brings in a speaker who does not deliver on the promises they made to the audience, they are going to hear it from the audience. Even worse, they will lose their audience for future events.

You can see that the stakes are high for event planners and organizers, which is why it can be very tricky to get speaking opportunities—paid, and even unpaid ones.

And yet, you are the kind of speaker they want on their stages. Your commitment to making a difference and your integrity around your own expertise are exactly what they are looking for in speakers. They just don't yet know that you are the answer to their search for a speaker. You are going to need to convince them.

Which means you need to start by offering to speak, even at the risk of them declining your offer.

One of my successful founder clients has a mantra: "No just means not yet." It's a mantra I hear in various forms from all of my most successful clients. I've been ignored and told "no" by many meeting organizers, as have all of my clients. In fact, my most successful speaking clients tell many stories of being rejected repeatedly on their path to success. There is no shortcut for most of us. There is only the commitment to keep showing up and offering to serve.The most valuable thing you can do to get on those bigger more influential stages is start exactly where you are, with audiences available to you right now, and blow them away with your ridiculously awesome content and engaging delivery.

The most valuable thing you can do to get on those bigger more influential stages is start exactly where you are, with audiences available to you right now, and blow them away with your ridiculously awesome content and engaging delivery.

Be willing to start on smaller stages and grow your influence from there.

Fall in Love with Serving Your Audience (at Any Level)

Make a commitment right now to let go of the idea that you must be on the big stages for it to be worthwhile. Instead make a commitment to serve in the most powerful way possible for the audiences most available to you right now. This includes dream speaking opportunities that will come your way as well as the smaller ones that make you wonder whether they are worth it. Take some time to ask yourself how you can love this audience. Is there a way you can serve—and be served as well by learning as much as possible—by this opportunity?

It doesn't matter if your audience is quite small. In fact, my most financially lucrative talks (which brought me many high-paying clients) have been in the smallest rooms because we get to dive deep together during my talk delivery and discussion facilitation. Depending on your goals, you may want to target small but extremely aligned audiences.

I'm not advising you to take any and all speaking opportunities. In fact, speaking for an audience that is outside of your Ideal Audience Member profile can mess with your sense of confidence and clarity because they may not "get you" at all—and you probably won't "get them" either. What I am saying is, ask yourself if you can take this opportunity to serve and use it for other goals you may have beyond attracting new clients. These goals might include: practice speaking; a place to get speaker reel by bringing in a videographer; an opportunity to get great still shots of you speaking; or a way to get awesome testimonials for your speaker page.

Speaking of your speaker page on your website, you really must create one.

HOW TO CREATE A COMPELLING SPEAKER PAGE ON YOUR WEBSITE

Your speaker page is where meeting organizers go to assess whether you are a good fit for their events. You want to make this page crystal clear and exciting to them. Here are the things to have on your speaker page:

- **Talk titles and descriptions:** Make sure the talk titles are ones that will delight the meeting organizers at events you most want to serve. Use your audience analysis exercises from this book to help you with this.
- **Images of you speaking:** The brighter and more engaging, the better. Be creative in finding these kinds of images. If you don't have photos of you speaking, use a great headshot so they can see your full face and get a sense of your energy.
- **Video of you speaking:** This is ideal, but I realize you may not have it yet. Make it a goal to get video at your next speaking gig. You can cut that video into the very best highlights and it will be a valuable resource for meeting organizers as they assess your fitness in speaking for their group.
- **Speaking Testimonials:** Even a few great testimonials about your communication style from credible sources—a leader in your company? A respected community leader with whom you have volunteered?—can make a tremendous difference in helping you get speaking opportunities.
- **Video interview or other media where you share your message.**
- **Publications or anything that shows your thought leadership in your industry.**
- **Names of events and organizations where you've spoken in the past.**

Before you decide you have to bail on this whole thing because you don't have an interview of you with Oprah, let's be clear: the more of these items, the better. Anything you can offer to the event organizer that helps them feel confident in your ability to light up their audience is very useful.

That said, don't let your desire to have an amazing speaker page stop you from getting one set up. Start with what you have right now. Even if you just have talk titles and descriptions, get those on a page and put a picture of you on that page so people can see what you look like.

There is a good chance you can get a testimonial or two even if you haven't done a lot of formal speaking. Colleagues, community members and friends who have heard you speak at meetings—at work, in the community, at the PTA—can all speak to your ability as a speaker. Be honest, of course, but be creative.

The goal of your speaker page is to help the meeting organizer get a clear and compelling sense of what it is like to be in your audience. A secondary goal of your speaker page is to let the meeting organizer know that it will be easy to work with you.

On my book resource page, **beyondapplausebook.com/resources**, you will find a speaker page checklist that you can download. Use that to guide you in creating your speaker page as soon as you can.

BE CLEAR FOR YOURSELF ABOUT THE OUTCOMES YOU WANT FROM YOUR SPEAKING EVENT

At the heart of every talk you deliver as a transformational thought leader is the deep commitment to serve your audience, to inspire hope and offer strategies through your stories, lessons learned, and expertise. But this isn't the only reason to speak. You might also speak to attract new clients and more speaking opportunities, to grow the community and grow your visibility in your area of expertise. You do this because you know that the more you grow and expand, the more people you can serve with your message.

In any one talk for any one audience, you may have different goals. These depend on the audience, the "rules" of this venue (for example, whether you are allowed to offer your services) and your own business model. You may not work with clients one-on-one or in groups—your business model may be solely as a paid speaker. You may be speaking to attract funding and volunteers for your nonprofit. Or, you may be in a phase in your business where you are growing your audience but don't desire additional clients because you are booked solid or in a transition phase with your attention on other aspects of your work. All of these things affect your goals for speaking.

Spend a few moments clarifying the outcomes you want from each talk before you deliver it. The engagement you invite with audience members beyond this talk is inspired by these outcome goals.

Here are some examples of possible personal outcome goals:

- **Grow your email list community (invite them to a free opt-in gift)**
  One of the best ways to expand your reach and service with your message is to inspire audience members to join your email community. The most effective way to do this is to offer a free gift that is related to the talk you are giving which they will receive when they sign up through a page on your website. I once converted 75% of the people in a good-sized speaking room full of people into email community members using this strategy.

- **Expand your Facebook group (share the link and invite them into the group)**
  Another way to create a clear method of connection for people in your audience is to invite them into a private Facebook or other social media group where you can continue to serve them with tips, resources, and inspiration. To do this, share the Facebook web address with the group while you are together during your talk, ideally at the end of your delivery. You may even want to invite them to

take out their phones and visit that Facebook group as part of your conclusion. This way you don't lose a subset of the room who have the best of intentions but forget to sign up after your talk is over.

- **Attract new clients**

  A natural way to let your audience know that you work with clients, and, therefore, would love to have them as clients, is to "seed" your talk with client example and success stories. These stories have a two-fold benefit. They are nurturing for your audience, showing them that they are not alone in their struggle, as well as inspiring them with hope for resolution. Most importantly for this outcome goal, these stories give concrete examples of the kinds of clients with whom you work, helping audience members assess whether they may be a good fit as a client for you as well.

- **Invite more speaking opportunities**

  When you share quick, relevant stories about other speaking you've done, people in the audience who are involved in related events may be inspired to invite you to speak at their events. It's important to be careful about this so as not to insult the organizers of the event where you are currently speaking, and so that you don't come across as bragging, but an example or two can go a long way to spark ideas for future speaking opportunity connections. Of course, the simple act of being a captivating and inspiring speaker at this event also supports this goal.

- **Test out your ideas and get more comfortable with speaking**

  This is a great reason to speak at events that may not be full of your Ideal Audience Members but are a supportive and relevant audience. Many of my clients speak at small group gatherings from their college alma maters or at local networking events with this outcome in mind.

THOUGHT LEADERS CONTRIBUTE TO THE LARGER CONVERSATION— ON STAGE AND OFF

You want speaking gigs, of course, but don't forget about other forms of thought leadership: writing and publishing, interviews, podcasts, and related outlets.

Remember Dina, who you met in Chapter 5, which introduced the 5 C's of Transformational Thought Leadership? She is a school designer who worked on a highly innovative research project in school architecture and public health. As a result of this unique experience, Dina often publishes articles in industry magazines and newsletters and is asked for input and interviews in her industry. She also gets new speaking opportunities from many of the talks she delivers. She actually spends a great deal of her time flying all over the world, sharing her insights as a school designer as well as her experience as part of the innovative research team.

My friend, Ursula, started an awesome podcast called "Work Alchemy: The Impact Interviews" in which she interviews thought leaders who are making a significant positive impact in our world. Ursula has interviewed such well-known thought leaders as Seth Godin, Marianne Williamson, Todd Henry, and Martha Beck. This commitment on her part to bring these powerful stories to her Ideal Audience Members who are looking for inspiration and life lessons has earned her a place of thought leadership as well. Ursula makes a powerful impact through her Impact Interviews. Not surprisingly, Ursula also is a beloved speaker in her industry.

Of course, there are countless examples of books, papers, podcasts, and even new television style media shows that are part of an overall thought leadership strategy. Leaders like Brené Brown, Jonathan Fields, Elizabeth Gilbert, Glennon Doyle Melton, Donald Miller and Byron Katie engage in many types of media for sharing their message. These are some of my favorite guides. I invite you to check out what your favorite thought leaders are doing. I bet you'll find that they have a diversified thought leadership strategy as well.

These are examples of how thought leadership goes beyond just high-impact speaking in your industry. As you think about your own desire to serve as a thought leader, explore ways you can serve beyond the stage through other channels. Those experiences will serve your speaking as well as your overall thought leadership and, most importantly, the people you are meant to serve with your message.

EXERCISE: CREATE YOUR SPEAKER PAGE

If you haven't already, create a speaker page. Use the checklist and guide available on our book resources page **beyondapplausebook.com/ resources**. Don't let the list of options for what to have on your speaker page dissuade you from creating your page. Make your page the very best you can today. Then you are poised and ready to send event organizers to this page to consider you as a speaker for their event.

Chapter Thirteen

LIGHT UP THE AUDIENCE WITH YOUR DELIVERY

*H*ave you ever watched an episode of The Ellen DeGeneres Show? If you have, I bet you are already smiling just remembering the experience. From the silly but oh-so-current monologue she begins with, to her subtle groovy dance moves, she is captivating from the start. We sometimes watch Ellen for our family "movie" nights and she always delights, even across our family of three generations. Ellen is a great example of someone who is devoted to lighting up her audience with her delivery.

WAYS TO LIGHT UP YOUR AUDIENCE

You can have the very best ideas in all the world—life-changing ideas—but if they're hidden inside a boring or otherwise lackluster delivery, you'll never be able to make the impact you are meant to make.

And don't worry, you don't have to be Ellen to be engaging and transformational in your delivery (no one except Ellen is Ellen, of course, so that's great news for us all).

That said, nobody wants to deliver a boring talk, especially you. You want to make a powerful impact when you speak, the kind of impact that sets you up as a known thought leader. That's why you're here.

The problem is, you likely get very shallow and confusing information about how to share your ideas through speaking, especially in regard to delivery style. You may hear things about when to move your hands and how to gesture for maximum impact, as if just motioning a particular way has some kind of magic. As soon as you try to do this, you can feel how it plays out in an inauthentic way. You feel stiff and strange.

Yes, there are ways to move your body to create further impact—but this is an art more than a science. And in my experience, it is largely intuitive. It actually comes from a *state of being* in which you are connected to both your content and your audience in a deep and surrendered way.

Captivating delivery comes from a state of being in which you are connected to both your content and your audience in a deep and surrendered way.

From this place, moving your hands in alignment with your content or moving your body toward a person in the audience all makes sense to your audience. It is far more useful to work toward this *state of being* than to practice how to move your body or inflect your voice.

In your regular day-to-day life you don't have a lot of great examples of this kind of speaking. In the business world, too often you watch otherwise smart and dynamic people turn into boring automatons when they present. In the outside world the most well-known examples of engaging speakers are people like Tony Robbins, who bring more energy and leaping on stage in one talk delivery than most of us can imagine in our lifetime.

Fortunately, there are now TED and TEDx talks and other online sources that give you a wider range of talk delivery styles. Still, it can be hard to figure out where you fit in all of those popular delivery styles you see.

The magic is in delivering in a way that is very "you" but also honors the content of your talk and your audience members. It used to be that when you thought of speakers, you would only have political leaders, evangelical preachers, and motivational speakers like Tony Robbins as a reference. Now, there are endless examples of speakers online through ted.com and YouTube alone, and there are many more beyond those, too. A quick look around makes it clear that we don't have to fit into a particular style to be an influential speaker.

There are so many ways to be captivating when you speak. Consider a couple of examples to see what I mean. You can easily search for these speakers and talks online if you haven't seen them:

Steve Jobs' Stanford Commencement speech breaks a lot of physical delivery "rules," yet, it's almost inarguably captivating. You can find Steve Jobs' talk online through a quick search to see this example in action.

Have you ever heard Ekhart Tolle or Tara Brach speak? Both are followed by hundreds of thousands of people, yet literally, they break about seventy percent of the great speaking rules. They both have voices that are quiet and meditative, and their voice fluctuation has little variance. They are often sitting down and moving very little while they speak. Yet people's lives are changed every day by their online and live presentations.

At the other end of the spectrum, you have speakers like Brendon Burchard and Hans Rosling. Hans has a TED talk called "The Best Stats You've Ever Seen." Both of these speakers have wild energy where they all but sprint back and forth across the stage. In the case of Brendon Burchard, he's jumping up and down and clapping much of the time. Both of them also have hundreds of thousands (or millions even) of fans who love listening to them speak.

HOW TO LIGHT UP THE AUDIENCE WITH YOUR AUTHENTIC STYLE: YOUR EXPRESSION ÉLAN

Remember in Chapter 10 where you named your Expression Élan? These are the three words that describe you when you are communicating in your most natural, engaging way.

Well now is the time to kick that baby in! How can you activate even more of your Expression Élan when you deliver your next talk?

Go back to Chapter 10 and read over your words and the descriptions you wrote about them, including colors, phrases and images. How can you use those to add some extra "you-ness" to your talk?

I'll give you some examples:

- Wear a dress or shirt in the color or colors from your Expression Élan.
- Infuse the images and/or colors from your Expression Élan in your slides or as objects you use in your talk.
- As you refine the wording in your talk, use words that evoke the energy expressed in your Expression Élan.

Here are examples of how my clients have used their Expression Élan (in speaking and beyond):

- Revamped their visual brand elements (logos, websites) to add colors that feel more vibrant.
- Chose outfits for big speaking events in colors that make them feel alive and more themselves (many times; this is a popular one).
- Changed titles of their talks—and switched personal stories to ones that are more revealing and authentic.
- Woven words and phrases from their Expression Élan process into their content to spice up their talks.
- Used their words to help them choose types of amplifying aids. One client played upbeat music and added a dance party, consistent with her Expression Élan!

- Added imagery based on details of their Expression Élan on presentation slides so the slides felt more authentic and also became more visually pleasing overall.

I've had clients completely redecorate their offices and clean out their closets to better align with their Expression Élan. There is such power in naming, especially when you choose labels that empower you to be your best self. Let this tool serve you in your authentic, powerful expression in any way you can imagine. Overall, your Expression Élan is an invitation for you to be a more revealed and amplified version of your authentic self at your best.

ESSENTIALS IN SPEAKING DELIVERY

There are some great books filled with excellent tips on speaking. I highly recommend the book *TED Talks* by Chris Anderson and *Captivate* by Vanessa Van Edwards, both of which have excellent guidance on how to use your voice and body movement in speaking delivery.

My overarching advice on delivery is simple: manage your speaking anxiety (as a daily fear-releasing practice and when you are about to get on stage) and be the most natural version of your best social self possible. The chapters on speaking anxiety and connecting with your natural expression style will guide you on both of these.

From there, here are things to focus on for your delivery:

Your "Hello Smile." This is my favorite part of meeting a new audience. Just as you arrive at the front of the stage, stop and make direct eye contact with some of your audience members. Just look at them and smile. In your mind, say "Hello." They will feel this "Hello" from you and smile back. It is a wonderful way to begin your talk as you will feel more connected to your audience and they will also feel more connected with you.

Genuine eye contact. In almost every college public speaking class and organizational training I facilitate, someone shares the "great advice" they've heard about eye contact: Just look right above their heads. I cringe every time I hear this. Don't try to do this! First of all, I find it incredibly difficult to do. I try to do this as a demonstration at trainings and always fail. My eyes keep being drawn back to their eyes. This is because the eyes are where you find natural human connection, nonverbally. When you really see your audience, you can "listen" to them. It allows you to make shifts in your content to better meet their needs if you notice when their eyes and face say, "I don't understand" or when they say "Yes! I am so with you!" Please don't deprive yourself of this gorgeous treasure chest of valuable information as a speaker. This kind of communication and connection can bring such a sense of peace and a feeling that "we are in this together." I can tell you, after nearly thirty years as a speaker, eye contact is my favorite anxiety reduction strategy.

Eye contact is my favorite anxiety reduction strategy.

Move toward your audience: be with them. This might sound like some of that superficial "body movement strategy" advice I warned against earlier, but I definitely don't mean it that way. For this to work, you first need to get yourself deeply connected with the audience. This starts with your audience analysis process during content creation. Then, as you are coming upon delivery day, soak yourself in the needs and wants of your audience. Understand their world. Know the ways you will make their life better. From this place of high commitment and desire to serve, allow yourself to move toward them as you speak in order to be more connected.

From the moment you walk on stage, you set a tone—for your audience and for yourself. Actually, it begins before that when you decide how you will connect (or not) with them. Decide to be with them, this room full of humans. Then move your body toward them whenever you can, to listen, to emphasize, to help them know when something matters. This might look like walking into the crowd, like Ellen does in her TV show. It might mean moving to the furthest corners of the stage in order to get as close as possible the audience at the edges.

Use gestures and movement in a way that naturally supports your content. Gestures are one of the most important elements in great speaking. Done well, they add visual interest to your talk and help amplify your content. As you practice your talk, think about ways you can use hand and body movements to enrich a scene you are describing, for example.

You can use gestures in concert with amplifying aids, too. That flower you are showing your audience—bend down to the floor to show its early growth and move your body upward to show greater growth. Remember, our brains are highly visual.

Allow your voice to fluctuate in tone and change in pace. Feel into the content of your talk and then use your voice to share that feeling with your audience. This will require that you practice a great deal so that you know your content well enough that your attention is not on remembering as much as it is on powerful expression. This is one of the great gifts that practicing a lot will bring for you and your audience. You each get to experience your talk at a whole new level of rich tone and voice variety. This is such a pleasure for your audience, and helps them pay attention.

Voice variation also helps your audience manage their attention and energy. For example, when you:

Whisper: They will get quiet and lean in so they can hear you.
Pause: They will stop daydreaming and attend, wondering what just happened.

149

Talk louder: They will pay closer attention to find out what warrants this new intensity.

Sing: They will be delightfully surprised.

Use an accent. Be culturally thoughtful with this one as you do not want to appear to be making fun of any kind of accent in particular. Done thoughtfully, they will again be delightfully surprised and curious about what you are saying in this new unexpected way. I love to use this one in my corporate trainings when I give examples of confidence building strategies. It is rare, if ever, that my corporate audiences get to hear a facilitator start to talk with a cartoon-ish southern accent and it always brings them back to attention.

Manage your anxiety so you can surrender to your expression. In many ways, this one is the mother of all speaking delivery strategies. The biggest thing that may be blocking your greatest expression is speaking anxiety. So when you use strategies to manage that anxiety, you will be freer to engage all of the other strategies I share here.

Anxiety blocks connection and connection is the essential element of speaking that makes the biggest difference in the lives of others. That said, speaking anxiety is a normal and meaningful part of becoming a go-to speaker in your industry. It is best to simply acknowledge that speaking anxiety will be a part of your journey and put practices in place. This is why I love the IF Today... Practice I talk about in Chapter 15, as well as all of the other in-the-moment anxiety management strategies you'll find in that chapter.

AUDIENCES LIKE REAL PEOPLE

In the book *Captivate: The Science of Succeeding with People*, author Vanessa Van Edwards shares a classic research study in which the researchers (Elliot Aronson, Ben Willerman and Joanne Floyd) were looking to find out what people really think of others when they make a mistake. In this research experiment, the researchers recorded a guy humbly sharing his high score on an exam he took. In two different situations, they either had him knock over a cup of coffee at the end where the listeners could hear the mistake happen, or he didn't knock over coffee at the end. That was the only difference between the two recordings. So, here's the best part. After they listened, people rated the speaker on likeability and social attractiveness.

Guess what?! As long as the person is perceived as credible (note that he did get a high score on the exam), the audience liked the spilling version of the guy better. We love it when others are human, especially in public speaking.

We love it when others are human, especially in public speaking.

Remember this, as you move through whatever speaking anxiety you may be experiencing and do your best to give more of your authentic self on the stage. Audiences don't actually like slick speakers. They want you to have prepared well and know what you are talking about, of course, but they want you to be real and human too. Audiences like people who can shift it up on the fly, who can handle issues that arise, and who let us get to know more of who they really are. This experience is special in speakers because we often see people trying to be perfect when they present, which often ends up creating more distance than it does connection.

Of course, none of this will entirely remove speaking anxiety for most of us. There's a reasonable chance that's true for you. That's why I'm going to share with you my life-changing Releasing Fear process in the next chapter. Because, well, it changed my life. It just might change yours in an awesome way as well.

First, though, let's get your content in the best shape possible, including your delivery practice plan!

EXERCISE: ENGAGE AND ACTIVATE YOUR EXPRESSION ÉLAN

You'll recall from Chapter 10 that your most compelling delivery comes from using your most natural expression style. In that chapter you went through a process that helped you reveal what I call your "Expression Élan," the three words that describe you when you are communicating as the very best version of yourself.

Revisit your Expression Élan words here, and then put a plan in place for how you will use the rich outcomes you discovered in that exercise.

Write out your Expression Élan words from Chapter 10 in a line like this in your journal.

Using your notes from the exercise in Chapter 10, write out three ways you will use your Expression Élan to help you be even more authentic when you deliver your talks. These will be things like:

Wear my ruby red blazer and red socks as a nod to the fire in my natural style (one of my clients added red to her brand colors and her wardrobe after she discovered her Expression Élan!).

Rework my thought leadership talk to add poetry references in appropriate places to recognize my love of beautiful language and poetic life lessons.

Revise my talk introduction to share more details of my personal story to reflect my desire to be more transparent in my work.

Each of these statements refers back to a specific Expression Élan word and its expanded elements. Yours will differ, of course. The key is to use your Expression Élan words to make your speaking more engaging, real, and personally meaningful.

EXERCISE: PRACTICE YOUR TALK LIKE CRAZY

It is time to practice! Exciting, right? That means that you're far enough along in crafting your content, and you've blossomed it out enough, that you can start trying it out through practicing.

Here's the deal: great speaking, the kind that allows you to serve from the most influential stages in your industry, takes a lot of time, preparation and practice. That's just the truth of it.

> Great speaking, the kind that allows you to serve from the most influential stages in your industry, takes a lot of time, preparation and practice. That's just the truth of it.

In his book *TED Talks*, the head of TED, Chris Anderson, says TED speakers often practice 200 hours or more before one presentation. As a regular speaker myself, as a coach and especially as a TEDx coach, I can vouch for the amazing amount of time it takes to deliver a talk with ease and grace on talk delivery day.

But ask any committed thought leader whether the time and energy is worth it and you'll get a resounding, "YES!" It reminds me of how athletes talk about preparing for game day. There is something deeply satisfying about pushing yourself to find out what you are capable of in a domain that matters.

You want to make a meaningful impact with your message. You are committed to being a transformational thought leader. Preparation and practice are simply your training. Devote to it as a commitment to your Ideal Audience Member and you will be amazed by the side effect of deep satisfaction from contributing at the edges of your own brilliance along the way.

Here's your practice plan:

1. **Set your expectations accurately**. Allocate significant chunks of time to practice throughout your week. Start with four hours a week, or more if you have a talk coming up in the next week or two.

2. **Begin practicing before you're done preparing your talk**. Record yourself, listen, refine, and repeat.

3. **Practice everywhere**. Practice formally, standing in front of a room (or at least in a private space) where you can move and gesture freely. Also practice in the car, shower, on walks and runs. Deliver your talk to your dog and your neighbor, if they'll let you. Practice everywhere.

4. **Practice in the space where you will deliver if possible** (or somewhere that is as similar as you can get it). This allows you to get familiar with the physical environment such as the stage or speaking area, lighting and acoustics.

5. **When you have mental capacity but can't practice aloud (maybe because others are around and it will disrupt their concentration), visualize yourself delivering your talk**. Be as detailed in your visualization as possible, from the way the room looks from your seat before you get up to speak to the smells and sounds in the room. Walk yourself through every step, seeing yourself rise from your chair, walk confidently to the stage or front of the room and then through your entire talk. It may not seem like it, but this kind of practice is surprisingly similar in effectiveness to actual physical practice in which you move about and talk out loud.

6. **When you have practiced like crazy, know when to let it go and trust**. In the hours before your talk, stop practicing. Go for a walk

somewhere peaceful or inspiring and think about other things. Plan your next vacation or daydream exciting things you have on your vision board. This is the time to care for yourself, feel proud of your devotion to your ideal audience member, and trust.

Chapter Fourteen

INVITE THEM TO DEEPEN THEIR TRANSFORMATION BEYOND YOUR TALK

*E*arly in my business, I learned a painful but powerful lesson about integrity in speaking. I was sitting on an airplane looking at all of my sticky notes in my folder and excitedly dreaming of all of the workshops and events that I would be delivering over the next year. I had spent the last month in deep planning and anticipation of this upcoming three-day workshop. I had invested a large chunk of money and was now flying across the country for this event based on the exciting case study stories and big promises of this business "guru." All my dreams for a thriving business making a difference in the lives of others were about to come true.

Over the course of the next three days, I felt my heart sink into the pit of my stomach, right along with my business dreams. Every time I heard someone in the audience raise their hand and share an example of a marketing headline filled with fear and scare tactics, to the high-fives and celebration of the lead business "guru," I felt like throwing up. I kept looking around to see if anyone else was hearing what I was hearing, or feeling what I was feeling. I had used this guru's "home study program" to create a plan I was excited about, but as I sat there in that room, I knew that I would never use the tactics this person was teaching to bring that plan into reality.

By the end of the workshop event, when this guru was at the front of the room, literally sweating and flailing her arms and accusing us of not believing that she would give everything that she had to our success as workshop leaders, I was near tears.

I believe wholeheartedly that in all things there is shadow and there is light. I have a deep and abiding reverence for the tools and practices that I have learned across my lifetime as a speaking coach and a communication expert, including the powers of persuasion. These tools can be used for good and they can be used for harm. It's our responsibility to make the right choices. My experience at this workshop reminded me quite personally and in an indelible way how important it is that I am both a model for and a teacher of the responsible use of these strategies.

I never teach selling from the stage using hidden manipulation techniques. Drawing on scarcity and fear, offering enough just to make the audience ache but nothing to help them move forward with or without working with me, and sharing only the grandest outcomes stories without an honest look at what it took to get there are way out of integrity. So as you begin to think about how you can offer to serve your audience beyond your talk, know that at the heart of these strategies I share is a reverence for high integrity. I know you wouldn't have it any other way.

That said, if you do work with clients and you are open to attracting new ones when you speak, I deeply believe that the people in your audience deserve to know that you are willing and able to serve them both in that room and beyond. If you offer services that will help them solve their most painful struggles or meet their greatest desires, it's good and right to let them know that. It's all in how you do it.

If you offer services that will help them solve their most painful struggles or meet their greatest desires, it's good and right to let them know that. It's all in how you do it.

Let me tell you a story about thought leadership speaking offered with integrity and an open invitation for greater service.

I went to this conference looking for real solutions. I was ready to get out of overwhelm and I wanted an experienced person who could help me do it. I was feeling really frustrated trying to balance some huge goals, crazy awesome new business growth, my commitment to time with my family... all the things.

When Megan began speaking, I knew I wanted to hire her in the first five minutes of her talk. She was inspiring, practical, and generous. I immediately began listening for examples of ways she had helped clients solve problems similar to the ones I was having in my business. After hearing Megan describe transformations she had helped her clients experience that were very similar to the kind of transformation I was looking for—namely, to finally get a clear strategy in place for managing all of my current clients and stay on track with projects I had lined up for the next quarter—I was sold! I couldn't wait to talk to her afterward and ask if she was taking new clients.

This is a great example of a very effective and graceful client attraction talk. The best client attraction talks are full of a reasonable amount of useful information that you can take action on immediately, and exciting client examples that show you that what you are wishing for but haven't been able to create, is truly possible. They set the speaker up as a clear solution to a problem you desperately want to solve.

Megan's talk was perfectly designed to empower those who wanted to take action on their own to make real progress toward their goals. It was also well-designed to inspire those in the audience who were ready for more support to reach out to her to explore the options for working together.

Let's look more closely at what Megan did in her talk that worked so well, as well as other ways you can gracefully "seed" your talk with clues about ways you can serve beyond this talk. We've covered most of these strategies in other parts of the book. This is the perfect place to see how you can use these strategies in your next talk.

WAYS TO GRACEFULLY EXTEND YOUR CONNECTION BEYOND THE ROOM

- **Infuse your talk with client stories.** When your audience hears example client stories it clues them in that you work with clients, inviting those who are looking for services like yours to consider your services as a solution to their problem.

- **Be honest while inspiring hope.** You definitely want to share stories of transformation and growth that your clients have experienced. In order to be ethical in your speaking, you also want to reinforce the full picture. They had to work hard. They had to do the work. This doesn't mean you have to share every single detail that your clients had to go through to realize their growth, but sharing a balanced view of what it took to get there is the way to maintain integrity. It allows audience members to assess for themselves whether they are ready to do the work.

- **Mention different types of offerings.** Megan talked about her group programs and she also spoke about one-on-one clients. Since I knew that I really wanted one-on-one support, I was thrilled to hear about that offering. I also knew that since she had a group program, working with her one-on-one probably came at a premium, so I felt better prepared for the conversation we had around pricing.

- **Talk about your books or podcasts.** My friend Nancy Jane has written multiple books and has a podcast called Happiness Hacks. She invites audience members to dive deeper and to learn more through her podcast and reading her books. These are ways that she serves beyond the talk that aren't necessarily related to working with her as a coach or counselor (though she also attracts clients through her speaking too).

- **Offer them a free gift in an invitation to your email community.** As I shared earlier, I once converted 75% of a room full of 125 attendees to my email list by offering them a free gift that was directly related to the topic of my talk that day. As a result of that increased connection and my ability to nurture those relationships through my email list, I gained multiple new clients, and also had one client design and request a brand new group coaching offering for me to lead.

- **Invite them to your Facebook group.** Facebook groups are favorite places to go online for learning and collaboration. Consider inviting audience members to a private Facebook group as an easy way for them to engage with and learn from you as well as connect with other like-minded people. It's a simple way for your audience members to choose to continue and grow your connection.

- **Speak directly about your services.** Gracefully threading into your talk ways your audience can get support from you after your talk works beautifully for the longer game of nurturing a possible client relationship. Sometimes it makes sense to be even more direct. Maybe you have a workshop or retreat coming up that would be perfect for this audience and it would serve them to know about it. Or you know the people in this room would love your new one-on-one offering, especially when they hear more about how it works. It's possible to invite your audience to work with you without being icky or "salesy" about it.

Sometimes a direct offer or invitation to work with you makes sense in your talk. Always confirm with the meeting organizer that a direct offer is appropriate before taking this approach. Here are guidelines for offering your services as part of a transformational thought leadership talk:

1. **Design your talk in a way that shows you really get what the audience members are struggling with, and that you are uniquely qualified to help.** All of the strategies covered in this book are designed to help you do this, especially your "I Get It" Intro and your Story of Transformation.

2. **Deliver your talk with your own style and a focus on genuine connection.**

3. **Let the audience know at some point in your introduction that you will spend a few minutes at the end of your talk sharing a bit about your program or services.** Reassure them that the content you are sharing in your talk is designed to be highly useful completely on its own, and that your program or services are simply a way to get more support in the implementation phase.

4. **After you share the rich content that helps your audience begin moving toward their own transformation, let them know that you would love to work with those who want additional support through the implementation of this new learning.**

5. **Spend a few minutes sharing some of the details of your program with a focus on the outcomes they can experience if they do the work.** Tell them how to learn more and sign on with you.

6. **Offer to answer questions after your talk, or through a complementary call to discuss their needs and get any additional questions answered.**

7. **As you close your talk, stay connected with the whole audience, those who would like to work with you and those are not at that place.** Assure them all that what you have shared, if implemented, can truly help them transform their own struggle, whether they work with you or not.

8. **Thank your audience with a whole lot of love.**

Chapter Fifteen

RELEASING FEAR
(AND ANYTHING ELSE IN YOUR WAY)

I was sitting in my favorite orange velvet chair in my living room staring out into our wild backyard, heavy heart, and totally sick to my stomach. I had been in business for a number of years at this point and was exhausted from trying to figure out how to make it work. I had invested in a zillion different programs, tried every approach you can imagine, and quit my business multiple times.

I had worked in my business part-time, full-time, full-time and a half. I had taken off full summers—and longer—and had periods of working 12-14 hours a day. I had written and published books, multi-media programs, created hundreds of videos. I had worked with some fabulous clients.

But it wasn't working. I couldn't figure out how to make it work without totally handing my life over to my business. As a mother to three young girls, this was not an option of any interest to me. It's not exaggerating to say that I hated myself for being such a "failure."

Now there's so much I could say about exactly what wasn't working. I had clients—amazing clients! And I felt so passionate about what I was doing. But it just felt so hard, and I knew I should be helping so many more people and that it was supposed to feel easier, more "in flow."

This certainly wasn't the first time I had sat in misery about my work. Actually (and sadly), this angst had become pretty normal for me. But this time there was just this one difference: I decided to take a completely honest look at what was really in the way of making the impact I wanted to make with my work.

That's when I noticed something new, that I hadn't seen nearly so clearly before.

Somewhere along the way I had stopped sharing my stories and my deepest message. I was riding on a message that attracted clients, but that didn't express what I really wanted to say. Because of this, I felt conflicted about sharing my message and, ultimately, I subconsciously resisted sharing it widely.

When I looked even more closely at what was in the way of me saying what I really wanted to say in my work, I saw that it was fear. In fact, I was afraid of so many of the same things my clients were afraid of. I was afraid of sharing my personal stories and being judged. I had all of these beliefs about how I wasn't qualified enough, hadn't gone to the right schools, hadn't worked in the right companies in the right jobs... so many stories I played in my mind constantly.

All the while, there were so many other stories that were also true. I had taught more than 1,000 people how to be better speakers. I had facilitated training at some of the coolest—and largest—organizations in the nation. I had worked with so many executives, thought leaders and brilliant people doing incredible and often life-changing work in our world.

I had been speaking since high school. In college I walked around campus with a banana and a binder full of the many textures and flavors of condoms to speak to classmates about HIV and AIDS. This was some pretty courageous speaking I had done. Yet, somewhere in the last few years, I had become slowly paralyzed by fear.

The good news was, I knew that now that I could see what was really going on, I could tackle it directly. I had been a frequent and successful speaker in the past. I had spoken on behalf of many non-profit organizations, booked exciting conference speaking gigs, and had gotten fabulous college teaching jobs. Every single time I stood before a room full of people to share my ideas and facilitate a conversation, every cell in my body said "Yes! This!" I knew I could get back there.

So I decided I was going to do whatever it took to start sharing my stories and take a stand for what I really wanted to say.

It turns out it was harder than I expected. I had dug myself pretty deep at this point. I ended up spending nearly eight months completely focused on a fear-releasing practice. I'm grateful to say this process changed my life.

I started to love speaking again. I began teaching college again. I started a storytelling circle where I began practicing telling my own stories. I began teaching more in my business, including creating multiple new video series as well as an online speaking program. I now step into those speaking events with even more excitement and thrill than I did all those years ago. The most important part is that I committed to sharing my message the best way I knew how for the highest good I could see at any time. This book is one of the ways I honor that commitment.

The truth is, you can have all of the best expertise and life lessons in the world, but if you don't care for your heart and soul—if you don't do the work of releasing very real fears that get in your way—you can't share those valuable lessons and expertise.

And, to me, this is a worst-case scenario. There you are, full of stories, lessons learned, and powerful expertise–stuck and unable to share any of it. Many people go unserved. This can make you feel even worse about yourself than if you didn't have that expertise. It's hard not to ask yourself, "What the hell is wrong with me?!"

That's what I kept asking myself. And in case you ever run up against that question for yourself, I want to give you the tools that set me free. These are tools I still use today, as do many of my clients. I want you to have them because the world needs you out there shining your light and changing lives with your message.

The world needs you out there shining your light and changing lives with your message.

These are powerful fear releasing tools. Before we dive into them, it helps to take a clear look at fear as it relates to your greatest expression. There are two ways to address fear:

1. Understand your fear.
2. Implement strategies for releasing fear.

UNDERSTANDING FEAR

Entire books are written on fear, and yet there is still a struggle to get a full grasp on understanding and explaining it. Fear is one of the most complex and pervasive of our human experiences. I won't pretend to even touch the tip of the iceberg of fear here. However, given that fear goes hand-in-hand with doing big, courageous work like stepping onto stages with your message, it must be addressed. This way you will have the tools you need to move through fear when it threatens your greatest contribution through speaking.

My own experience with fear, and specifically speaking anxiety, helped me take a clear and focused look at the many faces of fear. The gift of having worked directly with more than 1,000 speakers in the last two decades has shown me that I am definitely not alone. Here's just a tiny sampling of the thoughts that I have had over the years, and have heard from hundreds of others, too, at every single level on the path of speaking and thought leadership:

- I don't know enough.
- I'm not expert enough.
- It's egotistical to think that I belong on these stages.

- Who am I to say I'm an expert on this or anything?
- What if someone laughs at me?
- What if I make a mistake on stage?
- What if I say something wrong and somebody calls me out on it?
- What if one of my high school friends is in the audience and they think that I'm a loser?
- What if that woman that I did that not-so-nice thing to in our twenties somehow finds me one day and stands up in the audience and tells everybody what a jerk I am?
- What if I bore them?
- What if I trip? I'm so clumsy.
- What if I talk too fast?
- What if I drip sweat down my face?
- What if they think I'm ugly?
- What if I'm clueless and everybody knows it but me?

I could go on, you know, but this is getting kind of embarrassing for me, and I'm hoping that you relate to enough of the examples above to know that you're not alone.

These thoughts, and the stuck feelings they caused inside me and so many of my students and clients are the reason I created the IF Today... Practice. This is the practice that I began after that morning in the orange velvet chair that changed my life and allowed me to begin sharing my stories, life lessons, and expertise in a much bigger way. Later in this chapter I share with you the process of the IF Today... Practice.

The Many Faces of Fear

There is magic in simply recognizing fear and talking about it. Bringing it into the light is one way to decrease its shadowy hold in your life and work.

It is also helpful to recognize that fear comes in many forms, and that understanding the nuances of fear can help you understand how to respond when fearful feelings arise. Tara Mohr does an amazing job of talking about fear in her book, *Playing Big: Practical Wisdom for Women Who Want to Speak Up, Create and Lead*. My jaw dropped when I read her descriptions of *yirah* and *pachad*, two types of fear that come from the Hebrew Bible which she learned through a writer named Rabbi Alan Lew. I'll summarize them here in my own words.

Pachad: The fear that comes when you worry about what could happen. It's about the unknown and worst-case scenarios. With public speaking, this shows up in all the ways you may imagine blowing it before you even arrive at the front of the room.

Yirah: The fear that arises when you come into significantly more energy and take up a greater amount of space, much like you do with public speaking and thought leadership overall.

Isn't this fascinating to think about in light of public speaking, or really any kind of highly visible activity, which is characteristic of thought leadership?

When I think of these two descriptions of types of fear, I can feel the part of my energy about speaking that is *pachad*, and I can feel the part that is *yirah*. Recognizing that I can embrace *yirah* and release *pachad* as much as possible makes the process feel easier to me.

As you read through the releasing fear practices in the next section, it may be helpful to think of the *pachad* element of any fear you have and imagine releasing that part specifically. While *yirah* certainly has big energy, I have found that when I pull the two apart I can embrace the energy of *yirah* in a way that actually serves me well and feels kind of zingy and exciting.

IMPLEMENTING STRATEGIES FOR RELEASING FEAR IN PRACTICE

In my years of speaking and coaching I have found that there are two ways to address fear as thought leaders. One is a consistent practice that keeps you more steady and peaceful day-to-day; and one is the acute practice you can use during specific times when your fear energy is situationally high. In this section, I'm going to share with you my favorite practices for both.

The IF Today... Practice

This is the practice that I created after that morning on the orange velvet chair in my living room. It came out of a combination of desperation and dedication to rising up again. I was truly sick of myself and I knew I needed to do something different than I had been doing up to that point. Essentially, I went back to all of my favorite teachers, guides and piles of self-help books, courses and workshop notes, and pulled out my very favorite strategies. I re-engaged the tools that I had loved when I first learned them but had let fall away. Then I combined them into a practice I felt I could actually do regularly. It was an experiment. It took a while to tease out the right elements, but it worked. I started feeling better immediately (these tools have that effect) but the lasting impact became more apparent after a few months of practice.

"IF Today" is an acronym for Inner Freedom Today. What I would think to myself each day when I began using this practice was, "IF Today I just take myself through this fear releasing process, I will be free to do the work my heart is called to do." That's what I thought about each morning as I grabbed my journal and headed into my office or onto my deck to do my practice. I never imagined I'd share this practice with others, but after the profound difference it made in my life, I couldn't keep from sharing it with my clients, and now you.

Here Are the Elements of the IF Today... Practice
In your journal or a notebook:

1. **Write out your vision in full detail.** Leave nothing out and reach far and wide with what you really, deeply want. This may be an overall vision for your life or it could be one element, like your vision for how captivating and engaging you will be in delivering your next talk.

2. **Write out the Beliefs, Stories and Thoughts (BST) that are feeding the gap between your vision and your reality.** These are going to be things similar to what appears on the earlier list I shared negative thoughts that come up about public speaking. Ask yourself, *"Why can't this vision be reality? What's in the way?"* And then just go for it with all of those dark and often secret thoughts your mind tells you in response to that question. Write them all down. Don't worry, we aren't going to let them just sit there. We're about to take away a whole lot of their power.

3. **Play with those beliefs, stories and thoughts (BSTs) to help you release them or detach from them.** This is where it starts to get fun. Based on Byron Katie's The Work, this process is about questioning those thoughts playing in your head, sometimes without you even realizing they are there. You are shining a light on those thoughts and trying on different versions of them, as a way to see what's really real. Ultimately, your goal is to create "space" around those thoughts—to make them less absolute and black and white. Statements like "I am a terrible speaker" get reframed into "I sometimes struggle to make my point clearly" or "I have had some speeches not go very well, but I've also had a few that went very well." When you give your thoughts language that isn't so painful to hear in your own head, it's easier to detach from the thoughts that don't serve you and your greatest expression. They have less power. Reframe each statement into another statement that is less painful, yet still true.

4. **Release the BSTs that are ready to fall away.** Once you have written out your beliefs, stories and thoughts in new language, you can take actions that allow some of the most difficult thoughts to fall away, to release their constant replay in your mind. My two favorite ways to do this are to go for a walk and imagine the words just literally falling behind me as I walk, tumbling down my back and onto the sidewalk or path or to turn on some good dance music and dance, imagining the words falling off my back.

This process may be hard to imagine without more detail—I realize it's quite unconventional—so I have included access to the IF Today... Practice, including the Playing with Beliefs worksheet in the book resources page at **beyondapplausebook.com/resources**. I'd love for you to try it and let me know what happens for you. This practice changed my life and I love hearing stories about how it serves other committed thought leaders, too.

WHY ARE PEOPLE SO AFRAID OF PUBLIC SPEAKING?

No one really knows for sure why public speaking causes such anxiety in the vast majority of people, but one theory makes so much sense I like to share it often. Here's that theory:

Back in the early days of human evolution, every-day survival depended on membership in a tribe. If someone was abandoned by their tribe or group, they would die. They would be killed by an enemy or an animal.

When we step away from the "tribe" and into the spotlight of sharing our vulnerable stories and best ideas, we risk being judged—and ultimately, potentially being rejected. In our primal brain, this possible rejection puts our lives at risk because we would no longer have the protection of the tribe in the face of danger.

This theory gives us a strong evolutionary reason for speaking anxiety. I believe if we each can understand this and accept that it is some old leftover element in the brain then it is easy to simply put tools in place to help manage that very natural speaking anxiety so that we each can contribute in the way that we are meant to contribute.

MOVING THROUGH SITUATIONAL SPEAKING ANXIETY

I was standing on a stage in San Francisco. It was completely dark all around me. The only light in the room was the spotlight shining down directly on me. I could see shadows of bodies in the audience, so I knew that the theater seats were filled, but I couldn't see any facial expressions. I was really nervous because I was about to do something I had never done before. I was going to be someone else on stage. While I had been myself on stage many times as a speaker and a college teacher, this time I had to be someone very different. I was going to be Sojourner Truth, the African-American women's suffrage activist, delivering her powerful, room-moving *Ain't I a Woman?* speech.

In the center of her speech, there's a series of three sentences. Each of these sentences ends with "Ain't I a woman?" It's loud and powerful. I was giving this delivery all I've got when all of the sudden I realized... I had no idea which sentence I was supposed to say next!

I couldn't recall if I had already said "Aint I a Woman?!" twice and was on the last one, or if I was just finishing up the very first iteration of this powerfully delivered phrase.

I stood there paralyzed.

I stared straight ahead into the audience grasping in my brain for anything, any clue as to what I had already said to help me get the rhythm again. But, my mind was completely blank. My heart was racing and my knees were feeling very, very weak. But, I stood there and waited for what felt like 43 years.

And, then somewhere off from the far-right corner of the dark audience, I heard a woman yell, "Yes, you are!" Suddenly, I was brought back into awareness. Something in that moment of hearing this woman send her love and support across the aisles of this theater in San Francisco shook me out of my paralysis and I finished the speech.

Now, I have no idea what I actually said. I don't know if I repeated the whole speech again, or if I only ended up delivering the start and the finish. What I do know is that I've never forgotten the lesson that I learned in that experience. That lesson is this: my audience wants me to succeed. We're in this together, me and the audience. I've taken this lesson with me into all of my presentations for the 20 years since that day on that stage in San Francisco.

Speaking Anxiety is Stealthy

Speaking anxiety is stealthy. It begins when we hear we have a talk to deliver. It shows up for each of us differently, so you may not even recognize that you're feeling speaking anxiety. It might come in the form of "I'm too busy" or it might come in the form of procrastination. I even have clients who have a history of dismissing important upcoming talks as something they've got "handled" and, therefore, they don't need to prepare.

One client who is a seasoned speaker and successful business owner had the important and valuable realization during our work together that her speaking anxiety was actually masked in overconfidence and, therefore, led to a lack of preparation. And, while she was reasonably successful in her speaking, she always walked away from her talks knowing that she could have had so much more impact, and wondering what it would feel like to deliver a talk at the level at which she was capable. It had never occurred to her that speaking anxiety might be the thing in the way.

I want you to have both the awareness of and the tools to move through speaking anxiety, so I'm going to share with you some of my favorite speaking anxiety strategies. You will find many more on the book resources page, which you can access at **beyondapplausebook.com/ resources**.

MY FAVORITE SPEAKING ANXIETY MANAGEMENT STRATEGIES

Belly breathing. This one is simple, you can use it all the time, and you can start practicing right now as you read this page. Simply draw in your breath, mouth closed, through the nose, take that breath past your chest and bring that breath all the way into your belly until your belly fills up and extends. Release that breath all the way through your mouth so that you let out even more air than came in. Do this three times. Start practicing belly breathing now, and use it before every talk, as soon as you hear that you have a speaking opportunity, as you walk up to the front of the room when you first begin, and any time during a presentation when you feel you need to collect your thoughts. Belly breathing is magical. I now use it every day, throughout the day, to help me stay calm and present in all parts of my life.

A heart of service mantra. Make this your mantra as you prepare and throughout all parts of your delivery: "This is not about me, it's about them and how I can help." Great speaking is about the audience, always. Taking the attention off of yourself works wonders. The best part is, this mantra feeds your soul because you know deep down it's absolutely true.

Prayer. Say this prayer: "May I please serve today?"

Positive visualizing. Close your eyes and imagine yourself up on that stage. See yourself walking confidently to the front of the room, shoulders back, face in a soft smile. Picture yourself looking at a few people in the audience before you begin, making genuine human contact. Notice how you are excited and your body is full of energy, as well as confident and committed to serving with your message. Take yourself through the fullness of your talk moving to different parts of the stage, making connections with people in the far corners of the room. Imagine closing your talk with impact and seeing the audience clapping, and smiling, and nodding, and shaking their heads in delight and disbelief. Watch as people stand in appreciation of your talk. Do this often and enjoy every moment of it.

Prepare and practice like crazy. There is nothing that will ease your anxiety more than working your tail off to craft the most awesome speech possible and practicing it over and over and over again until the words, the concepts, the heart and soul of your talk and the details of it live inside your body, heart and mind. Preparation and practice is the greatest gift you give to yourself and to your audience, and it will be the most powerful anxiety reduction strategy.

EXERCISE: RELEASING FEAR—THE IF TODAY... PRACTICE

This is the daily practice I used to release the deep-seated fear that kept me quiet and not serving at my highest level for years, which I introduced in this chapter. To get all of the details about how to use this practice in your thought leadership, go to the book resources page at **beyondapplausebook.com/resources**.

EXERCISE: LOVE LETTER TO YOUR IDEAL AUDIENCE MEMBER

Write a love letter to your Ideal Audience Member. Share all of the details about how they are feeling, and let them know you understand and they are not alone. Speak to their desire to serve others as well as their desire to feel the satisfaction of serving. Recognize their fears and say out loud the thoughts they think no one else understands.

Imagine yourself holding both hands of your Ideal Audience Member as you craft this letter, connecting with them in the way that only those who really get it are able to do. This letter comes from the place in you that makes this connection.

Begin your letter something like this:

Dear beautiful soul (You can also use a name if you'd like),
I know that right now it feels... (what is he or she feeling?)
I am so honored and grateful that I get to serve you with my message, my
stories, and my lessons learned...(you take it from here with your heartfelt
message for them)

EXERCISE: BELLY BREATHE, RIGHT NOW AND OFTEN

Practice belly breathing every day. Use it all the time. Train your body to breathe this way. I promise you this will change the way you feel in almost all high-stress situations in your life. I use it in traffic. I use it with my kids. I use it with my dog, my neighbors, and even to help myself fall asleep at night sometimes.

WHERE TO GO FROM HERE

Dear Beautiful You,

We've come to the end of our time together here. It's such an honor to have spent this time with you to share my own experience, lessons-learned and stories. I'm so grateful for your commitment and your desire to serve with your message. I know that this way of life has intensity and it asks us to share ourselves and put ourselves out there in a way that can feel like too much at times.

I also know that this is a commitment we each make. It's a heart and soul thing. We have to remember that this kind of work chooses us, but that doesn't mean we have to answer the call. That's the choice we make and the commitment, too. I know it's scary and you doubt yourself at times. Me, too. But we can't ever forget the honor that it is to impact the lives of others in the ways that we can. We were invited to serve in this way. It's our gift and our honor. Learning how to impact others with your story and your message isn't easy. Many of us stumble through this learning, spending years, tons of energy, time and money. (That's my story for sure.) And that's okay because even those difficult experiences are worth it. But if what I share with you here on our journey together can shorten that timeframe and get you out there sooner making a bigger impact on more lives faster, then I've answered my call, too.

The truth is you can do this on your own. You can follow what's in this book and if you apply even half of what I've talked about here, you will have a tremendous impact on the lives of others. You will become recognized and known as a thought leader, and you will enjoy so many of the fruits of that kind of devotion and work in the world. You will have more clients. You will be offered speaking gigs. You will be invited onto podcasts, and you will be able to serve in ways that you dream of.

Here's what I also want you to know... you don't have to do this alone. I did it alone for the first decade of my career, and while some pretty amazing stuff happened, my major growth and impact, and ability to serve flourished dramatically when I started gathering with others who also doing this kind of work. That's what we do together in Your Rooftop Message Talk Speaking Program. I want you to know that we are here for you if you decide that you don't want to do this alone. We can craft your talk together. We can make your thought leadership plan. You can get the emotional, practical and other kinds of support with us.

Whatever you decide to do, please know that I am cheering you on with my whole heart and soul. I know that there are so many lives that will be powerfully impacted by your message and your willingness to share it, so please go climb that ladder, step onto that rooftop, cup your hands around your mouth, and let them know you're here, that you can help, and that you're ready to serve.

With love and deep care,
Michelle Barry Franco

ACKNOWLEDGEMENTS

I am able to take a confident stand for the ideas in this book because of the courageous and brilliant work of my speaking and thought leadership clients. My greatest gift as a speaking coach is that I get to learn from each of you. Thank you from the center of my bursting heart. The difference you make in our world inspires me every day.

To my husband and partner in all things, Jim, there is no way I can possibly thank you big enough for your support on this project and in every aspect of my life. I'm so grateful to share life with you.

I'm unbelievably lucky to be Mama to Serena, Annika, and Simone, each of whom bring so much delight and fascination to my world. Your interest and encouragement have made this book writing process a whole lot more fun. I promised you I'd thank Timber, the Big Black Dog, for his many hours of napping in my office, his steady breathing like a mantra: "keep writing, keep writing, keep writing…"

I'm blessed with a large family, which has taught me how to use my voice, even when chaos abounds. Thank you to my parents Dave, Chris, and Leone for being supportive and loving, each in their own ways. My siblings Greg, Angie, Kehau, Tina, Aaron and Adam keep me honest and humble, whether I like it or not and are each pretty wonderful people. Special thanks to Aaron for many conversations that have shaped ideas in this book, and his guidance on cover design. To my big brother Dave, in the

the world beyond this one, for always inviting me to sing at the top of my lungs. You showed me it was okay to enjoy hearing my own voice.

My mother-in-law, Norma (Grammy) deserves her own special shrine for all the ways she supports me and our family as we ride the roller coaster of creative work.

My mentors, coaches, and beautiful colleagues have all helped me hone and refine the content for this book, either actively or as part of our deeper work together. Heartfelt thanks to Angela Lauria whose brilliant program guided me to write the first draft of this book in record time and with incredible clarity. Big thanks also to Megan Flatt, Jenny Shih, Tara Mohr and Grace Kraaijvanger and The Hivery Community, all of whom have been tremendous support for me in the last few months and years as these ideas have become clearly defined and ready to share. My friends at Marin Storytelling Circle, especially Jacquelene and Arlene—this book would not be written, especially in this way, without you. I can't go without sending deep gratitude to Anneli—our work together is changing my life in ways I couldn't have imagined. Tam, I'm so grateful to you for the hours of listening and support for the ideas in this book, and everything else.

David Provolo delivered on cover design beyond my imagination, with invaluable help from two of the most creative people I know, Aaron Barry and Jane Selle Morgan. My editor, Kelly Lydick, turned a pretty good book into something immensely more useful and interesting to read and I'm so grateful. David Provolo delivered on cover design beyond my imagination. Adina Cucicov is forever a delight to work with and always surprises me with how lovely the pages of a book become in her care.

Most of this book was written on a series of writing retreats in the sweet yellow cottage on Molly's property in Sebastopol. Thank you for providing such a warm and comfortable writing home for me.

Finally, my wonderful colleagues and clients who allowed me to share their stories—their names grace these pages throughout. Your stories made this book infinitely more useful and engaging. Thank you for your willingness to share your stories in service of others. You're truly awesome.

REFERENCES

Introduction

1. Stuckney, H. & Nobel, J. (2010). *The Connection Between Art, Healing, and Public Health: A Review of Current Literature.* American Journal of Public Health, 100(2): 254–263.

2. Sullenberger, C. Sully Sullenberger: Author, Speaker, Safety Advocate. website: **http://www.sullysullenberger.com/speaking/**

3. Winfrey, O. (Podcast host). (2017, August 7). *Brené Brown Part 2: Living with a Whole Heart. Oprah's SuperSoul Conversations* [audio podcast]. Retreived from **http://www.supersoul.tv/**

Chapter One

1. Gilbert, E. (Podcast host). (2016, September 23). *"Show Up Before You're Ready" featuring Glennon Doyle Melton* [audio podcast]. Retrieved from **http://www.maximumfun.org/shows/magic-lessons**

2. Robinson, K. (2006, February). *Sir Ken Robinson: Do schools kill creativity?* [video file]. Retrieved from **https://www.ted.com/talks/ken_robinson_says_schools_kill_creativity**

Chapter Four

Examples of thought leadership stands:

1. Achor, S. (2014, November 10). Shawn Achor on happiness as a competitive advantage. Retrieved from **https://www.youtube.com/watch?v=jp9u2H_b71Y**

2. Brown, B. (2010, June). The Power of Vulnerability. [video file]. Retrieved from **https://www.ted.com/talks/brene_brown_on_vulnerability**

3. Cain, S. (2012, February). The Power of Introverts. [video file]. Retrieved from **https://www.ted.com/talks/susan_cain_the_power_of_introverts**

4. Mohr, T. (2014, November 13). Tara Mohr "Playing Big" Keynote—The 2014 3% Conference. [video file]. Retrieved from **https://www.youtube.com/watch?v=jCT6Ua-Znv0**

5. Sinek, S. (2009, September). How Great Leaders Inspire Action. [video file]. Retrieved from **https://www.ted.com/talks/ simon_sinek_how_great_leaders_inspire_action**

Chapter Seven

1. Sinek, S. (2011). *Start with Why: How Great Leaders Inspire Everyone to Take Action*. New York, NY: Penguin.

Chapter Ten

1. Cabane, O. (2013). *The Charisma Myth: How Anyone Can Master the Art and Science of Personal Magnetism*. New York, NY: Penguin.

2. Jobs, S. (2011, October 8). *Steve Jobs introduces iPhone in 2007*. [video file]. Retrieved from **https://www.youtube.com/watch?v=MnrJzXM7a6o**

3. Perel, E. Esther Perel Website: **www.estherperel.com**

Chapter Eleven

1. Ambady, N. & Rosenthal, R. (1993). Half a Minute: Predicting teacher evaluations from thin slices of non-verbal behavior and physical attractiveness. *Journal of Personality and Social Psychology, 64 (3)*, 431-441.

2. Anderson, C. (2016). *TED Talks: The official TED guide to public speaking*. Haughton Mifflin Harcourt, New York.

3. Brown, B. (2010, June). The Power of Vulnerability. [video file]. Retrieved from **https://www.ted.com/talks/brene_brown_on_vulnerability**

4. Heath, C. & Heath, D. (2008). *Made to Stick: Why some ideas survive and others die*. Random House: New York.

5. King, M.L. (1963, August 28). Martin Luther King—I Have A Dream Speech—August 28, 1963. [video file]. Retreived from **https://www.youtube.com/watch?v=smEqnnklfYs**

6. Medina, J. (2008). *Brain Rules: 12 Principles for Surviving and Thriving at Work.* Pear Press: Seattle.

7. MIT News: Massachusetts Institute of Technology. (1996). MIT Research—Brain Processing of Visual Information. Retrieved from **http://news.mit.edu/1996/visualprocessing**

8. Parischa, N. (2010, September). *Neil Paricha: The 3 A's of Awesome.* [*video*] *Retrieved at* **https://www.ted.com/talks/neil_pasricha_the_3_a_s_of_awesome**

9. Paul, A. M. (2012, March 17). Your Brain on Fiction. *The New York Times.* Retrieved from **http://www.nytimes.com/**

10. Sandberg, S. (2010, December). Sheryl Sandberg: *Why We Have Too Few Women Leaders.* [*video*] *Retrieved from* **https://www.ted.com/talks/sheryl_sandberg_why_we_have_too_few_women_leaders**

11. Stephens, G.J., Silbert, L.J. and Hasson, U. (2010) *Speaker–listener neural coupling underlies successful communication.* Proceedings of the National Academy of Sciences of the United States of America, 107 (32), 14425–14430.

12. Taylor, J. (2008, February). My Stroke of Insight. [video file]. Retreived from **https://www.ted.com/talks/jill_bolte_taylor_s_powerful_stroke_of_insight**

Chapter Twelve

1. Gladwell, M. (2008). *Outliers: The Story of Success.* New York, NY: Little Brown and Company.

Chapter Thirteen

1. Anderson, C. (2016) *TED Talks: The Official TED Guide to Public Speaking.* New York, NY: Houghton Mifflin Harcourt.

2. Aronson, E., Willerman, B. & Floyd, J. (1966). *The effect of a pratfall on increasing personal attractiveness.* Psychonomic Science, 4 (6), 227-228.

3. Brach, T. Tara Brach Youtube Channel: **https://www.youtube.com/user/ tarabrach**

4. Burchard, B. Brendon Burchard Youtube Channel: **https://www.youtube.com/channel/UCySH3WVP-5d4aJIfn8-WoPA**

5. DeGeneres, E. The Ellen Show website: **https://www.ellentube.com/**

6. Jobs, S. (2005). How to Live Before You Die Stanford Commencement Speech. Retreived from **https://www.ted.com/talks/ steve_jobs_how_to_live_before_you_die**

7. Rosling, H. (2006, February). The Best Stats You've Ever Seen. Retrieved from **https://www.ted.com/talks/hans_rosling_shows_the_best_stats_ you_ve_ever_seen**

8. Tolle, E. Eckhart Tolle Teaching Youtube Channel: **https://www.youtube. com/user/EckhartTeachings**

9. Van Edwards, V. (2017). *Captivate: The Science of Succeeding with People*. New York, NY: Penguin.

Chapter Fifteen

1. America's Top Fears 2015. **https://blogs.chapman.edu/ wilkinson/2015/10/13/americas-top-fears-2015/**

2. Katie, B (2002). *Loving What Is: Four Questions that Can Change Your Life*. New York, NY: Penguin.

3. Mohr, T. (2015). *Playing Big: Practical Wisdom for Women Who Want to Speak Up, Create and Lead*. New York, NY: Avery.

4. Truth, S. (1851, May 29). Ain't I a Woman? Speech. See this resource for translated text of Sojourner Truth's speech. Retrieved from **https://www. thesojournertruthproject.com/compare-the-speeches/**

ABOUT THE AUTHOR

*M*ichelle Barry Franco helps mission-driven founders and leaders make a big and beautiful impact by speaking on the best stages in their industry. She has individually coached more than 1,000 speakers over the last two decades.

Michelle works one on one with executives, founders, coaches and wellness experts to help them step into thought leadership through high-impact speaking and make a difference for as many people as possible with their message. In 2017 she launched *Your Rooftop Message Talk Group Program* and began offering private retreat intensives.

Michelle has a Master's Degree in Speech Communication Studies, an undergraduate degree in Biological and Cognitive Psychology, and has been informally but passionately studying body language and non-verbal communication since she was born. Her Whole Person Coaching certification is from Coach Training World. After working in a wide range of industries from insurance to high-tech start-ups to non-profits, and more than a decade teaching college-level public speaking and communication courses, she started her communication and speaking coaching business in 2008.

She lives in West Marin County, California with her husband, three daughters, one big black dog, and six hilarious chickens. You can find her at: **michellebarryfranco.com**.

BONUS THOUGHT LEADERSHIP
READINESS ASSESSMENT

*I*t's an honor to serve you and your message and I can't wait to see and hear your magnificent voice for good even more big, bold and courageous in our world.

Throughout this book I share the website address for our book resources page. In case you didn't want to break your flow, here's that link one more time: **beyondapplausebook.com/resources**. On that page you will find titles and descriptions of my favorite speaking, mindset and fear-releasing books, links to websites, videos and so many other resources that will help you use speaking to make the biggest difference in the lives of others.

On that page, you will also find my new ***How ready are you to hit the stage? Assessment***. Through a series of questions based on the two main models in this book: The 5 Cs of Transformational Thought Leadership Model and The Path to Thought Leadership model, you will learn which areas you most need to focus on in order to fully step into your role as a Transformational Thought Leader. With your results, you'll also have access to a feedback report with actionable strategies to help you increase your readiness for the stage.

Between this book and the strengthening and action taking exercises you went through here—and tools and strategies from your assessment report—we'll be seeing you shine your bright light in a way that really does make your biggest most beautiful impact soon! I can't wait!

Made in the USA
San Bernardino, CA
16 June 2019